HAUNTED HOTELS AND GHOSTLY GETAWAYS OF NEW MEXICO

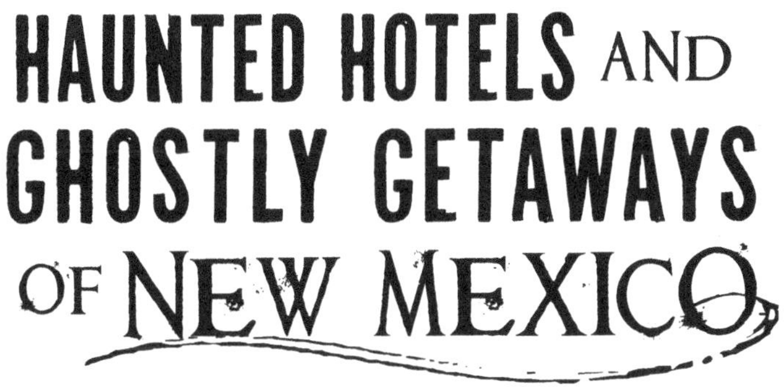

DONNA BLAKE BIRCHELL

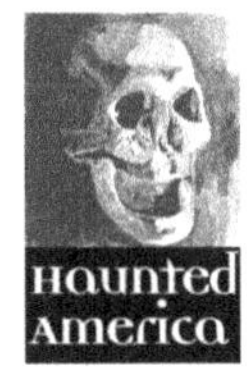

Published by Haunted America
A Division of The History Press
Charleston, SC
www.historypress.com

Front cover: courtesy of the author.
Back cover: Library of Congress; *inset*: courtesy of the author.

First published 2018

Manufactured in the United States

ISBN 9781467138895

Library of Congress Control Number: 2018942437

Notice: The information in this book is true and complete to the best of our knowledge. It is offered without guarantee on the part of the author or The History Press. The author and The History Press disclaim all liability in connection with the use of this book.

For all those who believe there is life after death
and are brave enough to seek it out.

For my beautiful mother, Dorothy Blake, who passed her sensitivities on to me,
I thank you for this amazing gift.

"Death is no more than passing from one room into another."
—Helen Keller

CONTENTS

ACKNOWLEDGEMENTS

Samantha Villa—your friendship started this ride, and I am eternally grateful!

For my family, Jerry, Michael, Sherrie, Justin and Amanda Birchell, without whose love and unending support I could not continue to follow my passion. Thank you all from the bottom of my humble heart. My cup overflows with much love and gratitude for each of you, since you all mean the entire world to me. Also, a huge thank-you to Robert and Missy Garriott for being such a great captive audience; so very glad we're family.

Many thanks to Jhett and Callie Sioux Schiavone of the Ruidoso folk rock band Gleewood (www.gleewoodmusic.com), whose CDs sang me through the many miles of this beautiful New Mexico countryside. Thank you for sharing your immense talents; you are both New Mexico treasures.

To my dear longtime friends Richard and Carol Estes, who are genuinely enthusiastic about these books and give me tons of encouragement. Carol, our road trip adventures to the hotels are something we will talk about for many years to come. Not to mention the exceptional wine. Many, many thanks! Love you!

To my work family at Mosaic Potash—Ashley Casey, Andrea Stanley Coley, Stacy Delgado, Jordyn Eaton, Nick Flores, Ricardo Hernandez, Anthony Ingram, Jillian Jaure, Susie Manquero, Peter Pavlik, Sandy Boyd, Ame Shirley, Marylou Gutierrez and Bill Dunn—who were constantly barraged with ghost stories. Thank you for your patience and pretending to be interested!

A huge shout-out to the tremendous efforts of my commissioning editor, Candice Lawrence, who threw up some obstacles during the planning of this book but always gave me a solution as well. I appreciate your kindness and patience. Also, to my new editor, John Rodrigue, who came in on the project midstream. To all of the staff of The History Press, for your outstanding help and expertise. Thank you for seeing it through to the end. You are amazing!

This book would not have been possible without the kindness of all the hotel/bed-and-breakfast owners, managers and staff who were more than willing to take time out of their busy days to humor a pesky author. Thank you for your enthusiasm, which encouraged me to forge on through adversity.

And thank you to you, the reader, without whom I would be nowhere. Please accept my deepest gratitude for your continued support and kindness.

All images are courtesy of the author unless otherwise indicated.

INTRODUCTION

Anyone who has ever stepped foot onto New Mexico soil will attest to the sheer beauty that gives our forty-seventh state the moniker "Land of Enchantment." You already know of the magnificent sunrises and sunsets that paint the azure skies, the snowcapped mountain ranges, vast caves, expansive deserts, rolling plains and lush waterways that make this piece of the United States such a unique landscape. I am proud to call New Mexico my home and want to share my little piece of heaven with you.

For those of you who are still unaware, you are cordially invited to tag along for the experience of a lifetime as we explore the many regions that comprise New Mexico, this time in pursuit of its historic yet haunted hotels. I challenge you to visit these outstanding hotels, not only to drink in the rich historical value of each but also to possibly meet some of the featured "permanent residents" for yourself by spending the night.

As a onetime skeptic, the idea of ghosts was something I scoffed at, stemming probably from being told all during my childhood, "there's no such things as ghosts." It wasn't until my own brief encounters that my mind was opened to the idea that maybe that saying was a bit wrong. It was with this enlightened mind that this project was born and gave me the curiosity to discover the possibilities of other worlds and dimensions. Please use this book as a guide to the rich history surrounding each of the establishments and its hometown by patronizing these beautiful properties.

Each story of the past lives most of these spirits experienced is heartbreaking; this may be the reason they have decided to continue residing in this world. Disbelief and shock as to their circumstances has garnered a refusal in them not to leave familiar grounds. Although our current world is much different than the one they experienced, they are still, in some cases, searching for loved ones and protecting their former homes.

I cannot promise that you will have an encounter or experience with any of the ghosts mentioned, but I can promise that you will have a wonderful time visiting their abodes.

INFLUENCE OF CULTURES

Ghosts, spirits and apparitions have always played a significant role in the folklore and legends that tie together the four great cultures that now reside peacefully in New Mexico.

The Native Americans have passed down stories for generations about their inhabitants of the spirit world. The White Painted Woman is credited with creation of the Apache peoples; the Changing Woman is said to have created the Navajo. Native American culture is full of spirits and folklore that is interwoven through their tribes.

As the Spanish/Hispanic influence grew larger in the Southwest, Christianity became more prevalent in the New Mexico Territory, overtaking the native ways mainly through force at first. The Spaniards' influence is seen throughout the state in the form of mission churches, chapels and cathedrals. The Spanish were also the driving force behind the beginning of the oldest wine industry in the United States. Mysteries and miracles relate to many of New Mexico's oldest churches.

Although insignificant compared to other cultures in the state, the African American community began to move west in large part to escape slavery. Many African Americans also migrated as part of the U.S. cavalry commonly known as the buffalo soldiers—a name given to them by the natives because of the resemblance between the hair of the soldiers and the hide of a buffalo (bison). The main function of the formation of the buffalo soldiers was to rid the West of the native peoples who were rebelling against the U.S. government. It is said that some of these soldiers brought the beliefs of voodoo with them as they made their journey west.

The Anglos' push west included eastern traditions originating in Europe, rounding out the fabric of the New Mexico Territory. Many of the new settlers were of Irish, Italian or German descent—cultures known for their healthy connection with the spirit world through fables, legends and religious beliefs. Early literary tomes of the nineteenth and twentieth centuries include stories of the spirit world in the West.

Each culture lent a hand in weaving together the diversity we enjoy in New Mexico today.

STRUGGLE TO STATEHOOD

New Mexico was under Spanish colonial rule from 1598, when Don Juan de Oñate developed the first settlement near present-day Socorro. Santa Fe was established as the capital city in 1610, making the City Different, as Santa Fe is known today, the oldest capital in the United States. In 1680, the native people revolted against the Spaniards, driving most of them deeper south into what is now the El Paso, Texas region, closer to the country of Mexico. In 1692, Diego de Vargas recolonized the northern area of what was to become the New Mexico Territory. These historical facts make New Mexico one of the earliest settled regions of the country.

Violence reigned supreme as the Land of Enchantment set out to establish itself as part of the United States. As a part of Mexico for many years, there were those in the U.S. government who questioned if the territory could, or would, be loyal to a new nation. Therefore, statehood was delayed. It would not be until January 6, 1912, that New Mexico officially and proudly became the forty-seventh state of the union.

NEW MEXICO TODAY

Surprisingly enough, to this day there are many residents of the United States who have no clue that New Mexico is part of the country. *New Mexico Magazine* runs a tongue-in-cheek monthly column titled One of Our Fifty Is Missing, which gives true instances of how the world perceives and, at times, is completely oblivious to New Mexico's existence. It is time to change this perception, and it is my hope that this book will help bring much-deserved attention to a beautiful state that offers so much to those who visit.

New Mexico is home to the International Balloon Fiesta, Zozobra, Route 66, Carlsbad Caverns National Park, Billy the Kid, horse racing, state parks and monuments, casinos, gorgeous sunrises and sunsets and, of course, world-famous green chile.

Many of the hotels in this book have been visited by mediums, ghost hunters and psychics who have each offered their own opinions as to the validity of the ghost claims. It is not the author's intention to verify any of these claims, but to tell, without prejudice, the tried and true colorful stories that each hotel has to offer.

It is the wish of the property owners for anyone wanting to conduct their own personal investigation to not disturb other guests, not bring Ouija boards, and please, always respect the policies of the hotel properties by contacting the owners or managers ahead of time with your intentions.

So, grab your cameras, suitcases and open minds and follow along as we explore the fascinating haunted hotels and ghostly getaways of New Mexico.

1
ALBUQUERQUE

HISTORIC ALBUQUERQUE

Officially founded in 1706 as a Spanish presidio, Albuquerque was originally a settlement formed on the banks of the Rio Grande by the ancient Tewa people, who inhabited early pueblos and have been recorded in the area for at least twelve thousand years. Evidence of these peoples has been found in the form of projectile points, adobe structures and petroglyphs, as well as other artifacts housed in the many museums in the modern city.

The Spanish conquistadors made an appearance in 1540 with the expedition of Francisco Vásquez de Coronado as they explored what is now New Mexico for gold and other riches. They found well-structured Puebloan farming communities. Within a few months of discovering these communities, the Spaniards forced the residents out and commandeered the structures and supplies for themselves, causing deep strife with the native people. Coronado would leave in 1542; following a fifty-six-year gap, in 1598, the next Spanish explorer, Don Juan de Oñate, showed up on their land to create more havoc.

Tired of being enslaved by the Spaniards, the Puebloan people rioted against their oppressors in the Revolt of 1680. Many Spaniards were killed as the Tewa people attempted to wipe out all evidence of the Spanish culture at their pueblo structures and surrounding lands. The Spaniards fled south to the Mesilla Valley, where they stayed for many decades until they finally braved the northern lands again.

Albuquerque started humbly and grew due to the railroad. It is through the railroad that many of its first residents came to the once desolate region. Railroad workers, businessmen and ladies of the night soon flocked to the tiny town in search of work. The red-light district flourished, which gave fits to the residents who fought hard to wipe this type of influence out of the town. Prohibition in the 1920s would do their job for them, and the district faded into history. The town expanded rapidly as construction began to radiate out from the Old Town area, where a few famous lawmen and outlaws could be still seen strolling the streets.

Early Albuquerque started out without a good zoning plan, so you will notice mansions across the street from hovels and a business in the middle of the residential area. This lent charm to the Albuquerque we know today.

ALBUQUERQUE TODAY

As New Mexico's largest city, Albuquerque is continually growing and expanding its boundaries. New subdivisions are being built almost daily as the consumer base strengthens. Home to huge industries and mom-and-pop businesses, Albuquerque has everything a person could want within the small subcommunities contained within the larger shell.

Old Town is a history buff's dream: a ten-block grouping of historical buildings erected around a central plaza. Included among these buildings is the oldest, San Felipe de Neri Church, which was built in 1793. Surrounding the church are adobe structures that were at one time private residences—now art galleries, restaurants and shops. The Plaza plays host to fiestas, parades and pageants. One quirky part of Old Town is the eighteen-mile-per-hour speed limit. Yes, you read that right—eighteen. The speed limit was originally installed because of Bicycle Boulevard in an effort to get drivers' attention to slow down for the bikes. There is also a scenic train ride available for your pleasure, and plans to include a trolley system much like the one used in the 1870s are said to be in the works.

The Albuquerque Bio Park and Aquarium/Zoo is located near Old Town as well. It gives visitors a full day's worth of activities, as does the Rio Grande Nature Center and Wildlife Refuge. The Bosque, named after the Spanish word for woodlands, runs along both sides of the Rio Grande, which divides East and West Albuquerque. This unique area provides residents and visitors with a multiuse area for biking, hiking, skating, horseback riding and running.

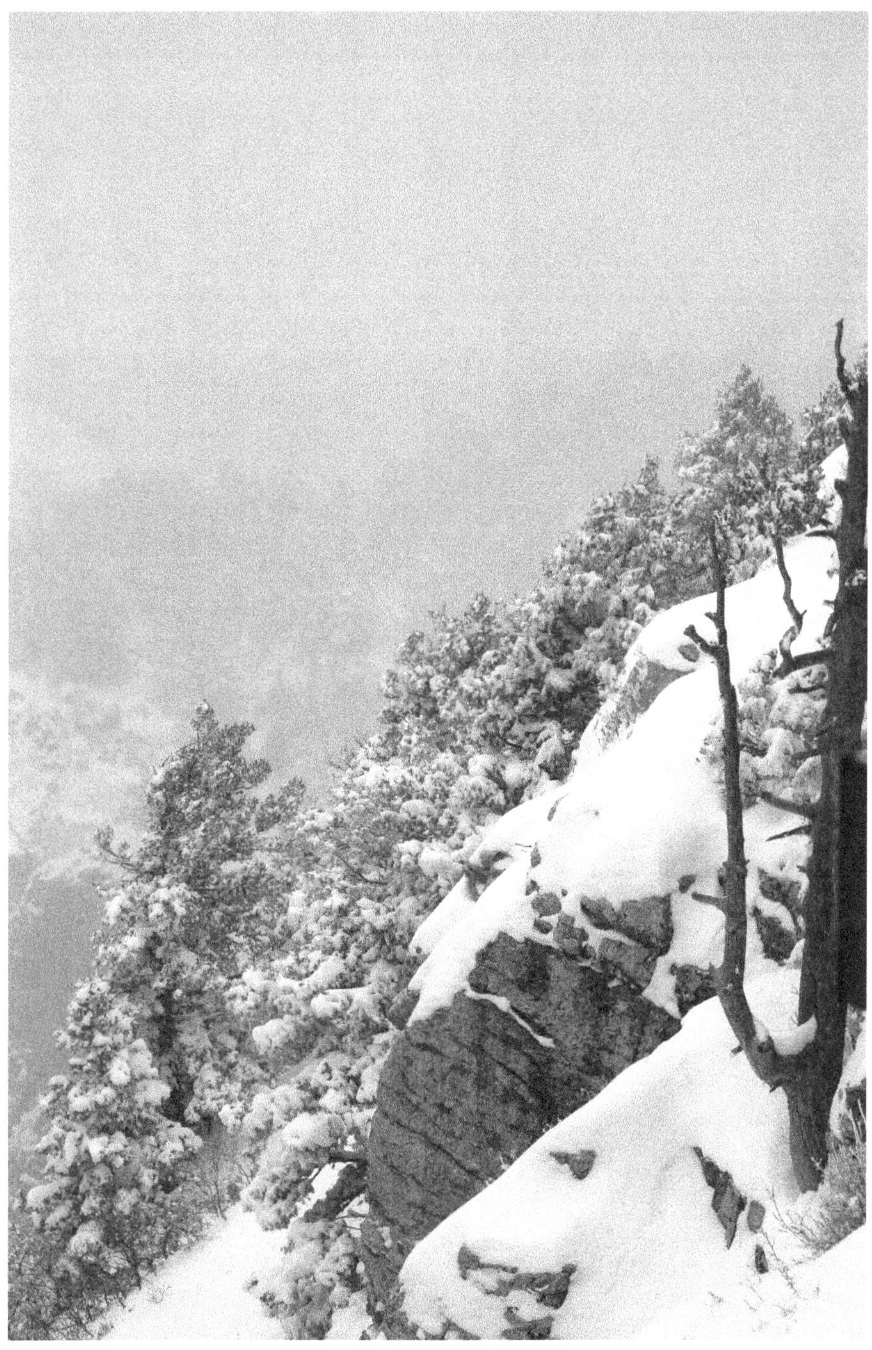

Views from the Sandia Tramway are spectacular. You will pass tall rock formations and towering pine trees on your 2.7-mile journey up the mountain. *Courtesy of the author.*

The Bosque is a protected area, the goal being to maintain its wilderness qualities as one of the world's largest cottonwood forests.

You always know you are traveling east in Albuquerque when the Sandia Mountains (Spanish for "watermelon") are in front of you. This gorgeous mountain range glows a pinkish red at sunset, hence the name. The Sandia Peak Tramway travels up this mountain range, giving visitors some of the best views in New Mexico. The tram travels 2.7 miles over deep canyons, climbing 10,378 feet to the top of Sandia Peak, and it is suggested that visitors try to time their trip to catch one of New Mexico's legendary sunsets. The tramway is open all year, closed only in high-wind situations. There is an eclectic gift shop at the bottom, and the trams are wheelchair accessible. A restaurant is slated to open soon at the top of Sandia Peak that will provide spectacular views to the lucky diners.

The Sandia Peak Tramway is the legacy of balloonist Ben Abruzzo, along with help from business partner Bob Nordhaus. It was built in 1966. The industrious pair also had a hand in starting Ski Santa Fe in 1984. Daredevils and ski enthusiasts, the partners were well known to skiers in the area. Members of Abruzzo's family are now real estate developers in the Albuquerque area.

Every October, thousands of visitors come to Albuquerque to witness a spectacular site: the International Balloon Fiesta, which began in 1972. Hundreds of brightly colored balloons, many with special shapes, take to the sky each morning of the fiesta after they get the "all clear" from the weather station. The beautiful azure skies are filled with bubbles of color as the balloons drift slowly over the city skyline in the brisk morning air. A crowd favorite is the Special Shapes Rodeo. To name just a few balloon shapes, there are motorcycles, stagecoaches, bumblebees, Star Wars characters, turtles, ducks, saguaro cacti, zebras, cows, suns, bulldogs and jesters. And yes, you will even see a pig fly! This is an event not to be missed.

West of the city proper lies the Petroglyph National Monument. It contains thousands of ancient petroglyphs carved into the basalt boulders and cliffs by the Puebloan people. This popular hiking area is easily accessible from a major road that separates the monument from nearby neighborhoods.

For nostalgic visitors, Albuquerque is a celebrated stop along the Mother Road, Route 66, which brought hordes of visitors into the city while introducing them to the Land of Enchantment. Historic hotels, with their eye-catching neon signs, lined the route along what is today Central Avenue. Several of the vintage hotels, like the Aztec Motel (the oldest), the El Vado Motel (built in 1937), the Tewa Motel, De Anza Motel, Luna Lodge and the

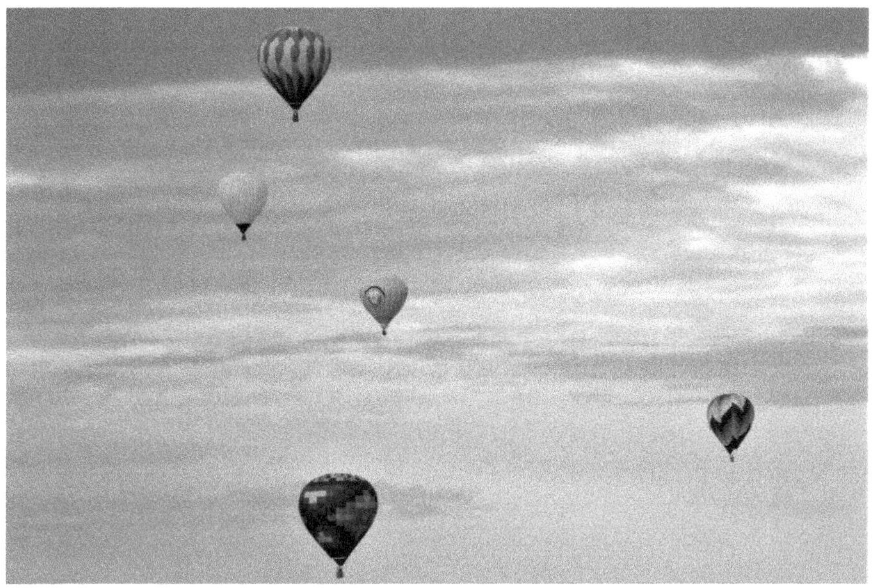

Hundreds of brightly hued and special-shaped balloons dot the morning skies as they participate in the International Balloon Fiesta, held the first week of October. *Courtesy of the author.*

Town Lodge Motel, still exist. Some are being renovated, so the area will be getting a much-needed renewal.

At the height of Route 66 in 1955, there were more than one hundred hotels along Central Avenue. It is said that travelers would have a tough time finding an available room. Today, Central Avenue is an eclectic mix of cultures and styles. The University of New Mexico is located on Central Avenue, so there are many coffee shops, pizza parlors, bike shops and unique eateries catering to students. There is a bohemian feel along the Avenue that ushered in the New Age movement with specialty shops, bookstores and yoga centers. It's also a great spot for thrift store shopping; you'll never know what treasures can be found.

As with the state itself, many cultures call Albuquerque home. This brings an eclectic blend of diversity for everyone to experience. The University of New Mexico is the hub of the Nob Hill area, which offers a wide variety of kitschy shops that appeal to the young residents and the young at heart. Restaurants of every description dot Central Avenue, some of which have been featured on Guy Fieri's Food Network show *Diners, Drive-Ins and Dives*. The Frontier Restaurant, across the street from the university, is a must-see, if only to try one of its world-famous cinnamon rolls.

THE PAINTED LADY BED & BREW

Located approximately one mile from Old Town, the Painted Lady Bed & Brew holds a good amount of history within its walls. A former brothel, grocery store and saloon, the Painted Lady could certainly tell some sordid tales. Restored and remodeled by owner Jesse Herron, cofounder of the Albuquerque Tourism & Sightseeing Factory that includes ABQ Trolley Co., Albucreepy Downtown Ghost Walk, and Duke City Pedaler, the Lady still has an air of mystery about it.

Taking up the better part of half a city block, the 135-year-old Painted Lady proudly stands its ground with native landscaping and private fencing. Owner Herron was described by the *Albuquerque Journal* as "one of the city's most prolific tourism entrepreneurs," and the Painted Lady Bed & Brew is a first of its kind. Albuquerque has seen an explosion of craft breweries in recent years, and Herron wants to capitalize on this by offering guests selections of local beer, "served in small quantities under a special bed and breakfast state liquor license." The Lady is also within walking distance of six taprooms and breweries.

Thought to have been built in 1881, the property was, as Herron put it, "a hidden gem" when he purchased it on February 3, 2014. He spent two years remodeling the site. A next-door neighbor found a signed board on his property dated December 12, 1897, which gives validity to the timeframe of when the Painted Lady was also built. It is also rumored that New Mexico's favorite boy outlaw, Billy the Kid, and the man who would eventually do him in, Pat Garrett, stayed there while in pursuit of the Kid, on separate dates, when it was a hotel before the Kid's death on July 14, 1881. Hotel registers are thought to exist that verify this fact.

Charlie's Grocery Store is owned and operated by Charlie Gonzales, who was the grandson of the original owner, Cesario Gonzales. The store and some low-income apartments once dominated the corner of Bellamah and Twelfth Streets. It is now part of the Painted Lady Bed & Brew property. Former owners also told Jesse that the site of the Painted Lady was once Native American land and was part of the Battle of Albuquerque, which took place near Old Town from about Fourth Street to the Rio Grande. There may be burials in the area. Herron had once considered tearing down the property when he purchased it, but the history fascinated him too much. Two years of lovingly remodeling the abodes resulted in a unique bed and brew for Albuquerque.

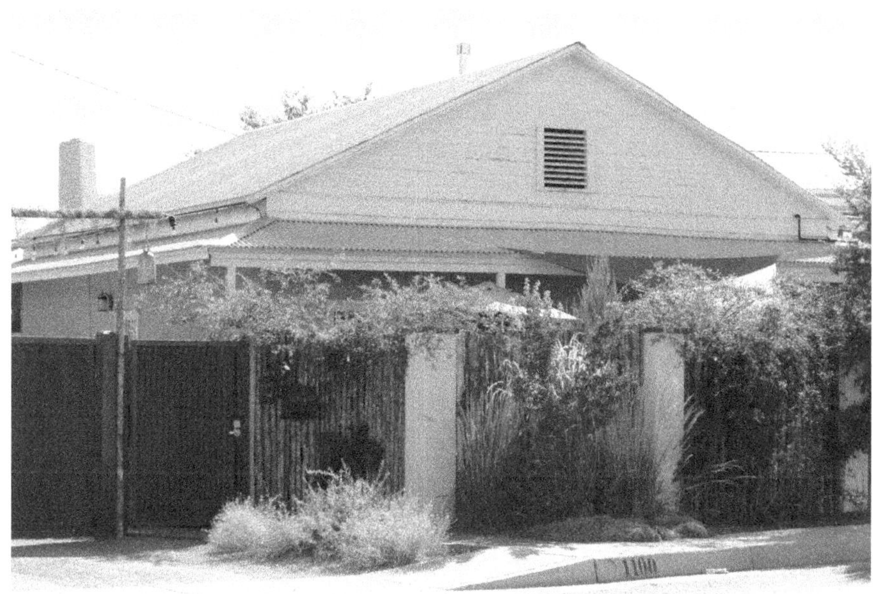

Above: Although this old girl has seen a colorful life as a saloon and brothel, the Painted Lady offers solitude in the heart of the busy city. *Courtesy of the author.*

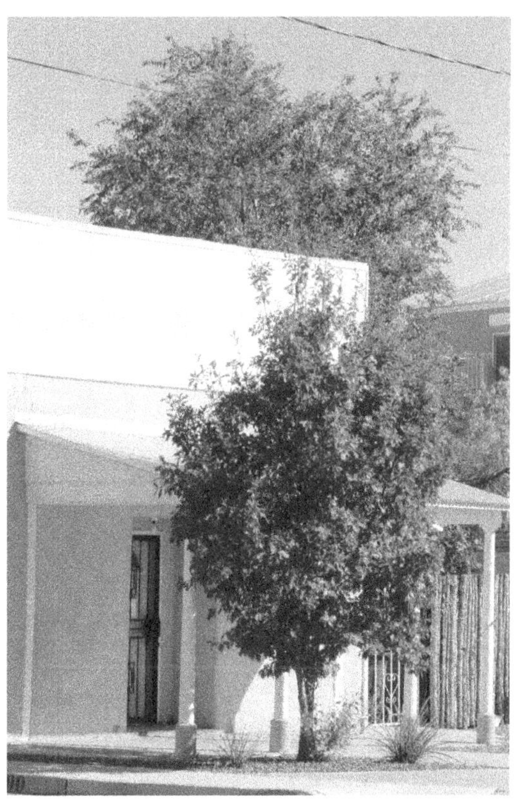

Right: Painted Lady Bed & Brew near Old Town Albuquerque is within walking distance of many fine breweries in the neighborhood. *Courtesy of the author.*

In a 2016 article for the *Albuquerque Journal* stating his reasons for opening his business in such a remote part of town, Herron states, "They want to be in somebody's home or a neighborhood where there's real culture, and not paying for parking or Wi-Fi or sharing the wall with somebody else. I think that's kind of where the trend is going."

When the Painted Lady was an eight-room brothel, it was conveniently located across the street from the American Lumber Company, which employed a lot of men. Each of the eleven-by-eleven-foot rooms had a window and a door that the ladies of the house would leave open to lure customers. There were a total of fourteen outer doors. A movable sign in front of the building was used to indicate a bar in the daylight hours and a brothel in the evening. The family that owned the establishment kept its business on the sly, and it is not mentioned in many of the newspaper articles written about the red-light district in the late 1880s and early 1900s, except for a brutal stabbing that took place in 1904 that sent four patrons to the jail and the hospital. Early newspaper articles were not clear as to the direct cause of the fracas, but when alcohol and women are involved, one can only imagine.

The connected bar was called the Swastika Saloon, for which the clientele developed a special drinking song. The former owners were bootleggers and moonshiners who made thousands of dollars in their trade. Since they did not trust banks, they would bury their money in coffee cans on the property. Jesse states that most of the money has already been recovered—but not by him!

The Swastika Saloon drinking song was originally written as follows:

When you heels hit hard and
Your head feel queer,
And your thoughts rise up like
The foam on a beer,
When your knees are weak and
Your voice is strong,
And you laugh like the devil at
Some d--- fool song,
Yer drunk, old boy, yer drunk
When you wake up in the morning and
You feel all in,
With a bursting head that aches like sin,
You feel in your pockets
Void of tin,

You'll probably say,
What a d---fool I've been.
Yer sober, by gosh, yer sober.

Jesse has been busy expanding his enterprise. He has purchased one of the original trolleys that was used in Old Town Albuquerque and that still had the old spelling of "Alburquerque" painted on the side. His plans include moving the trolley onto his property and turning the relic into "sort of a tap room for bed and brew guests." He has also purchased the old 1910 casita next door (a former bakery) and has plans to renovate this as well, to be used as part of the Painted Lady Bed & Brew.

The Painted Lady is open for business as of April 7, 2018, which is also National Beer Day, Jesse feels he will be able to bring even more of the authentic New Mexico to his guests. Guests will be able to enjoy the locally brewed beers, as they will be given a couple of pints when they stay.

Jesse is extremely proud to be able to embrace the enormous history of his property while bringing new life to the buildings. The otherworldly guests are just a bonus to the all-around atmosphere.

Ghosts

The owner's suite is the most haunted room of the house, and Jesse has experienced a variety of ghostly visits, from the comical to the hair-raising. The old owners described this room as "haunted as hell."

One story of a particularly menacing spirit will be sure to give you goose bumps. The legend states that a man found his wife with another man in the hotel and returned with an axe and proceeded to hack the couple to death. The spirit of the hacked man was still present when Jesse purchased the house. This room is said to be particularly disturbing to women, who are more sensitive; many of the former owners would not enter.

Also during this time, it seems everything was going wrong. There were problems with the renovations and the contractor—nothing was going smoothly. So, to stop what Jesse describes as a nightmare, he called in someone whom he describes as a kind of Buddhist priestess, who performed a cleanse on the home. She stated that there were three spirits in permanent residence in his apartment area of the home. The most menacing of them liked the corner and did not want to leave.

Although Jesse thought he had come to an understanding with the apparition ("leave me alone and I'll leave you alone"), he soon found out that the spirit wasn't going to live up to his side of the bargain and began to torment Jesse's three-legged dog, Bill Murray (Murray for short). This was too much as the dog was older and would yelp in pain and present bloody marks from apparently being bitten by something unseen.

Jesse called in a couple of local mediums who set up a demon trap for the spirit they identified as "Bill." Bill was described as in his forties, nicely dressed in the style of the late 1880s. The spirit did not leave quietly. but was eventually banished from the home. Jesse's dog, Murray, was immediately happy. Not to worry, Jesse assures that Bill is gone.

During renovations, Jesse's mother helped with the decorating. As they were preparing for guests, who were arriving later that day to go to the International Balloon Fiesta, his mother was taking the plastic off the brand-new refrigerator. She asked Jesse what he had said to her, to which he replied, "I haven't said anything." His mother laughed, reporting that she had heard a man ask her, "Can you grab me a beer?"

Another medium told Jesse that there is a ghost dog present in the home, which Murray has noticed. The ghost dog upsets Murray when the spirit messes with his food bowl.

On numerous occasions, Jesse has been, as he states, lucky enough to hear two men talking, an old piano playing, glasses clinking and sounds of the barstools dragging on the floor, no doubt residual sounds of the brothel.

A family member of the original builders told Jesse and his family that there are three ghosts who reside in the property. But, they were quick to say, they were "nice" ghosts. Jesse was told to expect to hear at approximately 12:30 a.m. each morning a "shuffle, shuffle, cane, jiggle." This is Uncle Charlie doing his nightly check of the doors to keep his guests safe.

RED HORSE VINEYARD BED & BREAKFAST

Nestled in the farmlands of the South Valley of Albuquerque, the Red Horse Vineyard Bed & Breakfast is a little piece of heaven. The moment you step on the property, you begin to take deeper breaths and look for the nearest easy chair to bask in the serene surroundings. At the Red Horse, they like to say that the time spent there is an experience—not just a stay. Guests have been quoted calling the Red Horse an "oasis in the desert."

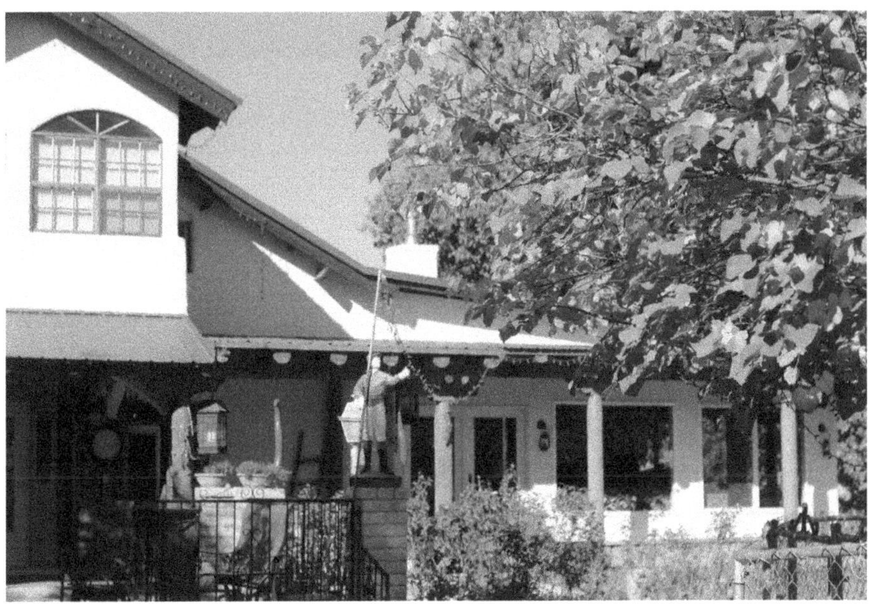

The red trim on the white house of the Red Horse Vineyard Bed & Breakfast is a tribute to Carl Londene's Swedish heritage. *Courtesy of the author.*

Built in 1870, the site was purchased by the Londene family in 1968, even though the structures on the property were in extreme disrepair. This was the only house in the area when the Londenes bought the property. The vineyard located on the front of the property dates to 1892 and had to be lovingly tended to produce the grapes the family uses in their wines. These precious grapes were brought to the New World from Europe when the Ellis family homesteaded the area in the 1870s.

A root cellar is now the wine cellar, filled with rare wine-processing equipment, such as a 1914 wooden grape press (the only one in New Mexico), which is still used today. This equipment is museum quality; in fact, the Londenes have been approached many times with offers to purchase the treasures, but all have been refused.

Carl Londene started making his own wine in 1969 and still has a few of his first run in the wine cellar. The first winery on the property was started by the Ellis family in 1912. Wine and apple cider have been produced on the Red Horse property since 1870, except for the twenty years when the second owners, the Winfields, owned it. The original grapes in the vineyard remain unidentified, but there are Concord and Cabernet Franc, which were used to supply mission wine to the area. There is still one white grape in the vineyard, which no one has been able to identify yet. It is the last to mature in September and is so sweet that no sugar is necessary to add to the wine.

In its lifetime, this property has been part of the Artrisco Land Grant (one of the few Spanish colonial land grants still in existence today), was a Neosho Pony Express turnaround station, had wagon train mule exchange corrals and was a campsite for the Confederate army during the short-lived Civil War Battle of Albuquerque.

During the Battle of Albuquerque, it is said that a cannon located on the Red Horse property in the Civil War era was fired from there to Old Town, some five miles away. The battle began on April 8, 1862, when rival forces led by Edward R.S. Canby of the Union army and General Henry Hopkins Sibley of the Confederate Texas Mounted Volunteers lobbed long-range artillery at each other for two days. The Confederates were on the retreat from the Battle of Glorieta Pass and occupied Albuquerque during this movement. The battle stopped when Canby was informed by a resident that the Confederates would not let the citizens take shelter.

Canby decided that his army had made its point and caused other Confederate factions to leave their posts to come to the aid of Sibley's forces; he left under the cover of darkness without being detected. Sibley ceased his occupation of Albuquerque on April 12, 1862, leaving behind his wounded and is said to have buried eight mountain howitzers and several cannons on the edge of town before retreating farther to Texas.

The remnants of the original wood and tar paper house finally collapsed in 1971, but the Londenes salvaged the wood from the structure and repurposed it throughout the property. There is an eight-foot-deep fish pond in the front yard of the Red Horse that was once the original wine cellar.

Another interesting building on the acreage is one of the three original adobe structures that once housed the *braceros* (Mexican farmworkers). This building had five rooms housing five to six people per room. Each room contained only one bed and a woodstove. The braceros were vital to the agriculture system of the region until a fire swept down the acequia (irrigation ditch) that connected all the farms and burned up the valley. The braceros were no longer needed in the valley, so they moved on.

The Red Horse Vineyard Bed & Breakfast is family run and operated. On most days, you will see the dynamic team of owner Carl Londene and his daughter Darlene and son-in-law Phil Capshaw working on some aspect of the B&B. Accomplished artists, father and daughter create beautiful works in ceramics as well as oil paintings. The ceramics, inspired by the owner's Swedish heritage, feature the red Dalecarlian horse, which originated in

Dalarna, Sweden, hence the name Red Horse. The wooden carved horse was originally used as a toy for the children of the villages but later became a source of livelihood for the wood-carvers who began the tradition.

Upstairs guest rooms have original wood paneling, and the downstairs has the original wooden floors. Although a recent addition, the game room makes use of the earliest windows from the collapsed structure. This way, the Londenes feel they are carrying on the traditions of the land and carrying it forward for the new generations. Each of the rooms and the hallways are graced by paintings done by Carl Londene as well as murals created by artist and family friend Sharon Higgins. Darlene reported she was honored to be asked by Sharon to paint the train in a mural in the bathroom depicting five generations of the Londene family.

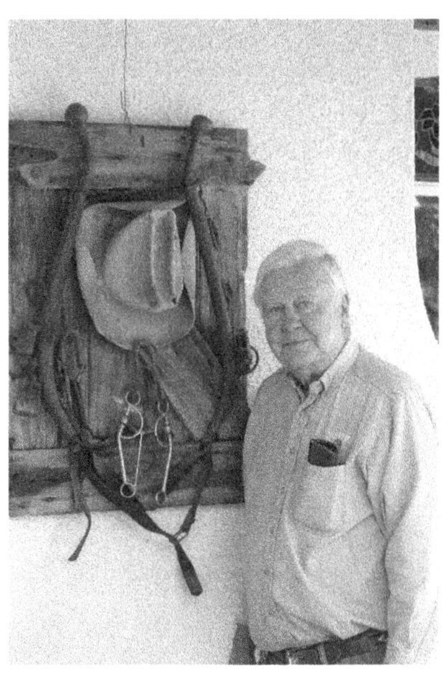

Hand-painted ceramic items are available for purchase at the Red Horse Vineyard Bed & Breakfast. Carl Londene creates vignettes from old tools and found items. *Courtesy of the author.*

A gift shop in the main part of the house contains a wide variety of their handiworks, including coffee mugs, bells, necklaces and earrings, gnomes and, of course, red horse figurines. The rooms of the bed-and-breakfast are adorned with many of Carl Londene's original paintings, setting the mood and theme for each room. As a rancher, Londene used many tools in his trade, and many of these artifacts have found their way into interesting vignettes created by the owner. Hats, chaps, lariats and spurs grace the quaint artwork.

Peaceful surroundings and grounds make the Red Horse a perfect venue for weddings, reunions, birthday celebrations and weekend retreats. You will feel instantly at home and welcome.

Mr. Londene's sense of humor is a delight, and the pride he has for the legacy he and his wife, Donna, have established is evident in his twinkling eyes. Although there is a huge hole triggered by Donna's passing in 2013, her welcoming spirit is still quite apparent in her loving family.

Ghosts

Carl Londene's late wife, Donna, was a sensitive and could feel the presence of the otherworldly. She would carry on conversations with beings no one else was able to see. This was quite normal for Donna, and it didn't bother her a bit. But for others, it was unsettling.

Two little girls in blue were some of Donna's favorite visitors. The girls would skip up and down the upstairs hallway, giggling as they played. Recent visitors to the Red Horse asked Darlene where the children were that were playing in the hallway. Much to their surprise, there were no children on the property at that time.

Another of the frequent spirits was a man dressed in Victorian clothing who would appear at the foot of Donna's bed from time to time. The two would carry on extensive conversations.

2

CARLSBAD

HISTORIC CARLSBAD

Carlsbad began life as Eddy, New Mexico, in 1888, named after its founder, Charles Bishop Eddy, a cattleman from New York State. If Eddy was created today, it would have been one of the biggest real estate promotions ever known. At the time, Eddy was founded on a wing and a prayer with the vision and drive of one man (Eddy), who accomplished an amazing publicity feat, attract people from around the world to settle in a flat piece of land in the middle of a desert.

It was Eddy's dream to have the perfect society free of vice of any kind—especially alcohol, since he was a teetotaler. As a former resident of Colorado City, Colorado, Eddy was determined to model his new venture after his favorite Colorado town. The saving grace for the region was the Pecos River, which Eddy saw as a huge asset and set out to literally cash in on its potential.

Local cowboys dubbed the area Rattlesnake Flats due to the extremely large population of rattlesnakes in the region. Running cattle through this rangeland was exceedingly dangerous, not only because of the venomous snakes, but also because of the snake holes, which could turn the ankle of a horse or steer in an instant. Rattlesnake derbies became a favorite sport in subsequent years and helped to clear out the reptile population considerably while raising money for local causes.

Investors and settlers alike were unable to resist Charles Eddy's charisma, and the town grew by leaps and bounds to become the county seat. Soon, the small hamlet in the southeast corner of New Mexico was home to immigrants from Italy, Switzerland and Germany. Due to one of the largest irrigation projects in the United States, contrived by Charles Eddy, Charles Greene, J.J. Hagerman and Pat Garrett (of Billy the Kid fame), the town of Eddy was an agricultural wonder. Crops of cotton, grapes, alfalfa and sugar beets, as well as orchards of peaches, sprang from the arid desert landscape to thrive and produce large yields.

Fruits and vegetables from Eddy County won multiple awards at county and state fairs, as well as at the Chicago World's Fair. The alkaline terroir of the soil made it possible for crops to flourish. Today, pecans, cotton and alfalfa are the largest products of the area.

Once the railroad came to Carlsbad in 1890, getting crops to market was much easier; the town truly became connected to the rest of the country. Carlsbad garnered its name after Charles Eddy left the town to start enterprises elsewhere. A spring that feeds into the Pecos River was found to have the same mineral contents as the healing springs in Karlovy Vary, or Carlsbad, a famous thermal springs spa in what is now the Czech Republic. The decision was made by founding citizens Robert and Mary Tansill, who had visited the healing springs abroad, to adopt the new name in honor of the mineral water.

Plans for a sanatorium, bathhouse, cabins and tent city at Carlsbad Springs were devised in 1904 by a newly formed company, spearheaded by local physician Dr. Doepp. Unfortunately, the bathhouse was the only structure ever built. The spring was the main source of fresh water for many of the new residents. In 1911, a petition was placed before the town board of trustees to change the name of Carlsbad to Carlsbad Springs, which failed.

In 1926, one of the largest deposits of potash was found east of Carlsbad by geologist V.H. McNutt, who was looking for oil when the core sample produced an equally valuable treasure. A residue of ancient forest fires, potash is primarily used as a fertilizer for crops because of its rich potassium content. This mineral discovery was especially important during World War I and World War II, since Germany was at that time the only source, and the country cut off supply to the United States. Potash has since supplied Carlsbad with a steady source of income and livelihoods.

Carlsbad flourished and would be home to the world-famous Carlsbad Caverns National Park, an Army airfield training bombardiers (including several classes from China) and German prisoner-of-war camps in World

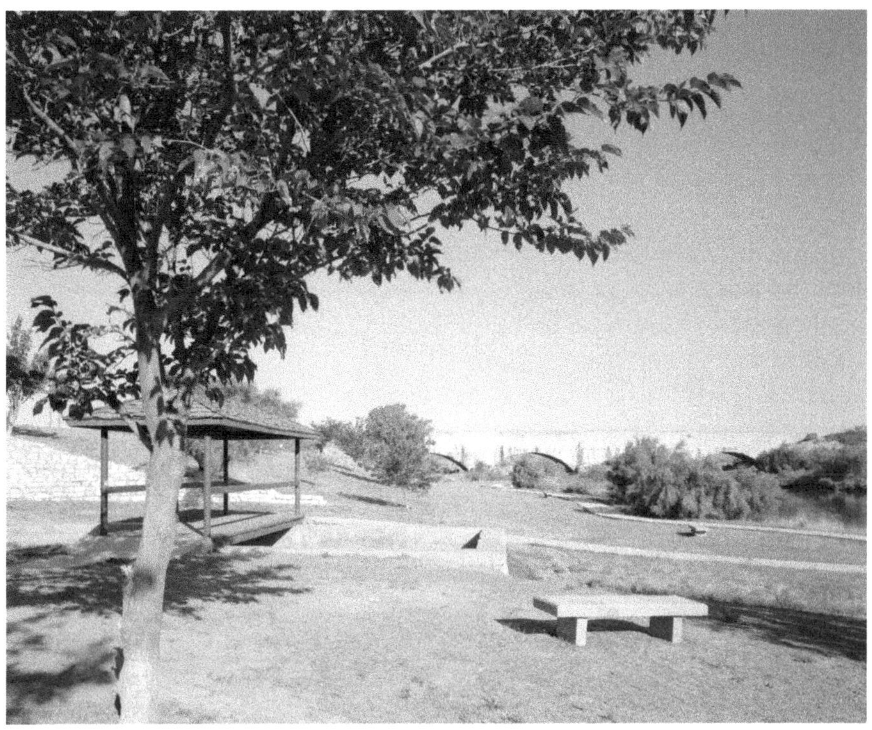

The Springs of Carlsbad were thought to have healing qualities. In 1891, the spring produced more water than what was used by Denver, Colorado. *Courtesy of the Southeastern New Mexico Historical Society.*

War II, plus many participants in the tragic Bataan Death March. A few survivors and their families still reside in Carlsbad today. Also, those who called Carlsbad home were well-known politicians, scientists, actors, artists, singers, writers, military heroes, astronauts, athletes, race-car drivers, oilmen and cattlemen.

Many would be surprised to know that actor Dan Blocker (Hoss Cartwright on *Bonanza)*, actor Bruce Cabot (*King Kong*), race-car driver Dick "Mr. Chevrolet" Harrell, famed artist Roderick Mead, baseball hero Cody Ross, Staff Sargent Barry Sadler (who wrote and sang the "Ballad of the Green Berets") and astronaut F. Drew Gaffney, to name but a few celebrated individuals, are claimed by Carlsbad.

CARLSBAD TODAY

Modern-day Carlsbad is fueled by tourism from the nearby Carlsbad Caverns National Park, which draws well over half a million visitors to the area each year, as well as the Living Desert Zoo and Gardens State Park, home to indigenous plants and animals of the Chihuahuan Desert, in which Carlsbad is located. There are also the potash mining industry, the oil and gas industry and the Waste Isolation Pilot Plant (WIPP) (a unique, safe nuclear waste depository), all of which provide an ample supply of employment for the region.

The Pecos River, which meanders through the heart of Carlsbad, is still the lifeblood of the region and continues to attract fishermen, boaters, walkers and swimmers nearly year-round due to the moderate climate the area enjoys. The city has installed a water park and splash pads for residents and tourists alike. Recent expansions include a splash zone for children and residents with disabilities called Friendship Park.

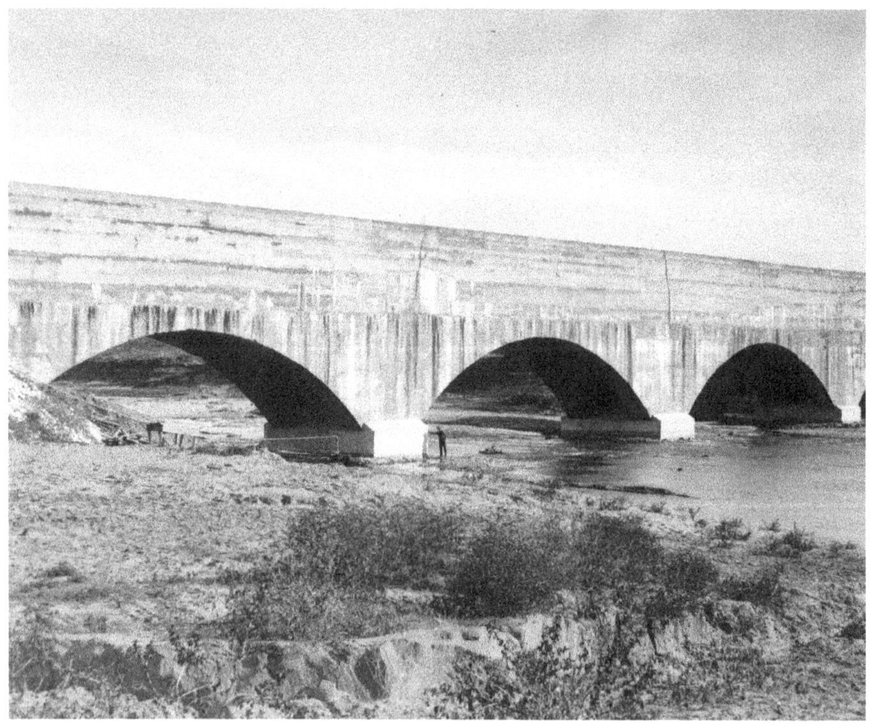

The Pecos River is the lifeblood of the Pecos Valley, providing much-needed irrigation to the arid landscape via a concrete flume. *Courtesy of the Southeastern New Mexico Historical Society.*

During the holiday season, residents who live along the banks of the Pecos River create magical light displays in their backyards for boat tours to view. This event, called Christmas on the Pecos, runs from the Friday after Thanksgiving to New Year's Eve. Nationally acclaimed for its beauty, the boat tours have become a favorite annual destination for many tourists. The event grows as more and more lights are added to backyards, bridges, golf courses and an island along the smooth Pecos River. The Carlsbad Navy provides the safe navigation of large party barges every night. Recently, helicopter rides have been offered to those who want to witness the splendor from the sky.

Sports play a big part in Carlsbad life; the Bob Forrest Youth Sports Complex was built to accommodate the many events the city hosts each year. These state-of-the-art facilities include fields for baseball, softball, football and soccer, as well as their own refreshing splash pads, which can be used any time, whether one has friends or family members participating in sports.

Carlsbad is home to several microbreweries, including Milton's Brewing, Guadalupe Mountain Brewing Company and the Lucky Brew, which bring in many wonderful musical talents from around the region while providing handcrafted beer to taste. Also, the Balzano family—owners of the Trinity Hotel—has a winery at their vineyard about twelve miles north of Carlsbad at Seven Rivers and has branched out to include an annual pumpkin patch with a petting zoo in the month of October and an antiques fair in November. The winery is also a beautiful wedding venue complete with a full-sized Cinderella coach.

As with most towns in the United States, Carlsbad has seen lean times, but its resilience has been inspiring. Its growth has always been steady, but Carlsbad is currently experiencing a boom due to the oil industry, which has attracted many new businesses to the Cave City. The once sleepy small town is now bustling with activity and easily triples in size during the workweek. It has a bright future.

The Trinity Hotel

Built in 1892, the Trinity Hotel started out as the First National Bank building and the home of the first newspaper for Eddy (soon to be renamed Carlsbad). Renovated in 2007, the two-story building was on the brink of disaster, appearing on New Mexico's "Endangered Historic Buildings" list before three partners took on the monumental task of bringing this magnificent structure back to its former glory. Previous office spaces are now nine beautifully appointed hotel suites.

In its rich history, the Trinity also served as an office site for Carlsbad (Eddy) founder Charles B. Eddy and Sheriff Pat Garrett. In recent history, it was the home of the Carlsbad Irrigation District offices. It was through a loan from the Revolving Loan Fund (RLF) and local support that the renovation of the historic building was possible.

"When my partners and I started on this project, we wanted to create something totally different in Carlsbad," said Dale Balzano, owner of the Trinity Hotel. "Without the support of the RLF Program, this project would never have come to fruition."

The owners of the hotel and restaurant, father and son Dale and Derrick Balzano, along with partner Michael Moore, in the words of Dale Balzano, painstakingly "adhered to the rigid standards of New Mexico and United States Department of the Interior for Historic Preservation to transform the crumbling edifice into the Trinity Hotel." The hotel now holds a proud spot in the National Register of Historic Places and has been thankfully preserved for future generations to enjoy.

Today's boutique hotel offers amenities including wine chillers, flat-screen TVs, docking stations, free Wi-Fi access, as well as the special plush Trinity robes. Some of the exquisitely designed suites include sunken bathtubs to bring even more luxury to a visitor's stay. The Victorian Italianate style of the hotel stands out against the surrounding mostly adobe/pueblo style of architecture on a historic corner in Carlsbad.

Free wine tasting is available in the Trinity dining room from 3:00 p.m. to 7:00 p.m. daily. This gives patrons an opportunity to taste the many spectacular wines not only of the Balzano Vineyards but also of the state of New Mexico itself. Boasting the oldest wine industry in the United States, New Mexico has some excellent, award-winning vintages that will be sure to please even the most discerning palate.

Janie Balzano, wife of Dale, serves as chef for the delicious menu the Trinity provides. Italian dishes dominate the wide selection, but delectable steaks and seafood are also available. New additions to the menu can be found each week, so visitors should go back often. These delightful plates can be paired with the Trinity Hotel's signature wine, The Spirits of Seven Rivers, as well as other New Mexico tasty wines. Breakfast and lunch menus are also available to start your day off right. Many of the dish names have historical ties to the Trinity and to the Carlsbad area.

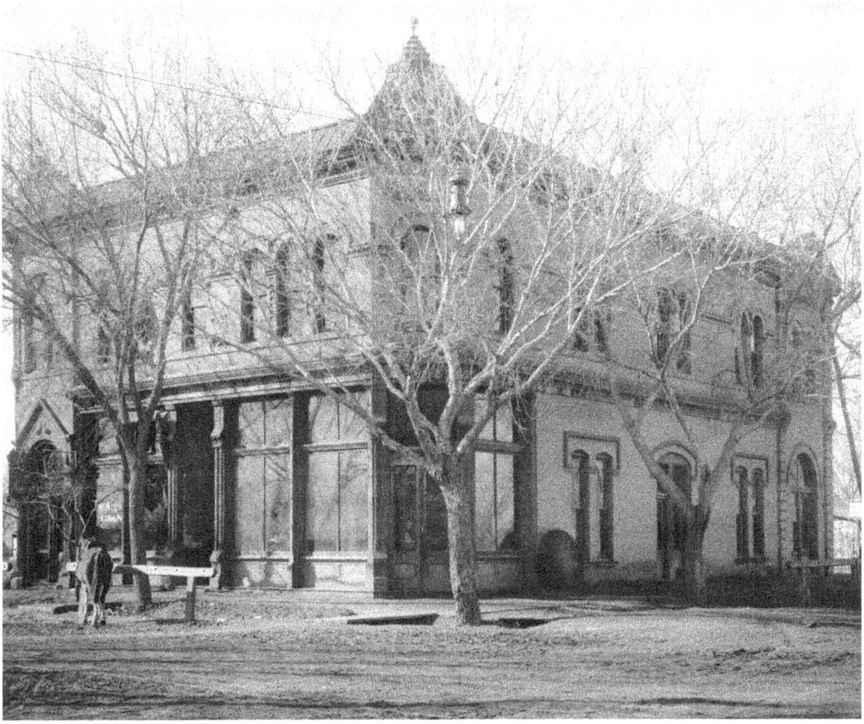

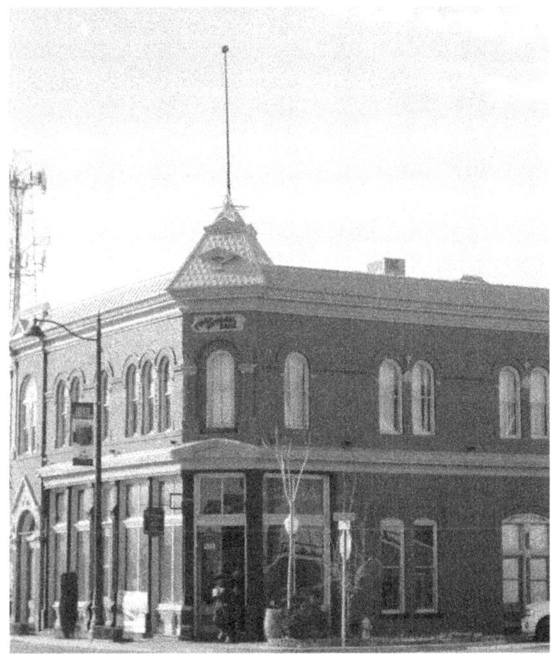

Above: The First National Bank building, shown in this 1905 image, now known as the Trinity Hotel, has seen Carlsbad grow from this corner since 1892. *Courtesy of the Southeastern New Mexico Historical Society*.

Left: The Trinity Hotel is one of the few remaining buildings in Carlsbad that dates to the 1800s. This hotel has stood the test of time. *Courtesy of the author*.

The Trinity Hotel gives back to the community is many ways, one being providing free Thanksgiving meals for anyone who wants one. This tradition was started by fellow restaurant owner Pete "The Chef" Panagopolous of the now closed Deluxe Café. He would prepare free Thanksgiving meals for all. Dale Balzano, owner of the Trinity Hotel, was quoted in a *Current Argus* staff article: "I was always struck by Pete Panagopolous' generosity, and I knew that someday I wanted to be in a position to give back to the community the way he did for so many years. This is our way of saying thank you to Carlsbad and thank you to Pete for the generosity of spirit that he exemplified through his giving."

Janie Balzano makes a delightful traditional meal of turkey, stuffing and dessert. She expects to feed at least five hundred people each year. It is certainly a labor of love.

Gleaming original wooden floors, pressed tin ceiling and heart-stopping crystal chandeliers welcome the many patrons of the Trinity Hotel. A massive mirrored-back bar sits directly in front of you as you enter the dining room from the lobby gift shop. You will be given the option of being seated downstairs or upstairs; both have excellent benefits. Downstairs, you are in the mix of things; upstairs, you get a bird's-eye view of the restaurant below. The resident ghost, Ruby, prefers the upstairs.

Ghosts

Miss Ruby has been making her presence known to the Trinity Hotel staff since the hotel opened in 2008. Generally hanging out in her favorite spot on the second floor of the restaurant in a secret room (be sure to ask your server to show you the entrance to this room), Ruby is said to patiently watch the staff as they prepare the tables for the day's patrons. She also has definite opinions on music and has been known to turn off the sound system when a song she deems offensive comes on. The friendly spirit also likes to call the staff by name.

Ruby is thought to be the former secretary of the Carlsbad Irrigation District around 1888. Her favorite room to haunt is 206 (which contains the vintage safe). It was also originally her office. Rooms 201, 206 and 207 were one big office during her time; the Balzanos sectioned them off to make the hotel rooms we know today. Ruby is still protective of her office space.

Ruby is also a prankster who likes to pick on single females who stay in her room. She is known to be very inventive in her pranks, as one guest reported to Dale Balzano. He told the owner that he and his family awoke one morning and looked for the towels in the restroom, only to find them on top of the window ledge. Mind you, these windows are approximately seventeen feet tall, with the sill being another two feet off the floor, for a total of nineteen feet. There was no means by which the towels could have been placed that high in the room. A ladder had to be used to retrieve the objects for the family.

Ghost hunters who investigated the property also told the owners of another spirit that resides there. This apparition is allegedly of a caretaker who worked at the Trinity building for forty years. The staff and owners call him the "Glass Breaker" because of his propensity to break glassware to show his disapproval.

Stories are also told of the hotel's vineyards, located twelve miles north at Seven Rivers, being haunted. Hence the reason behind the wine label, The Spirits of Seven Rivers. The Seven Rivers cemetery had to be moved due to the construction of Brantley Dam, a diversionary dam originally slated to cover most of the Seven Rivers area. Due to this disturbance of the graves, it is said that a cowboy on horseback will sometimes be seen coming through the wall of the grape-processing building. A little girl has been reported playing among the grapevines.

These reports ring true with the description of the graves as documented and relocated by an archaeological team. Seven Rivers has long had the reputation as being the most violent town in New Mexico (in the 1880s), and

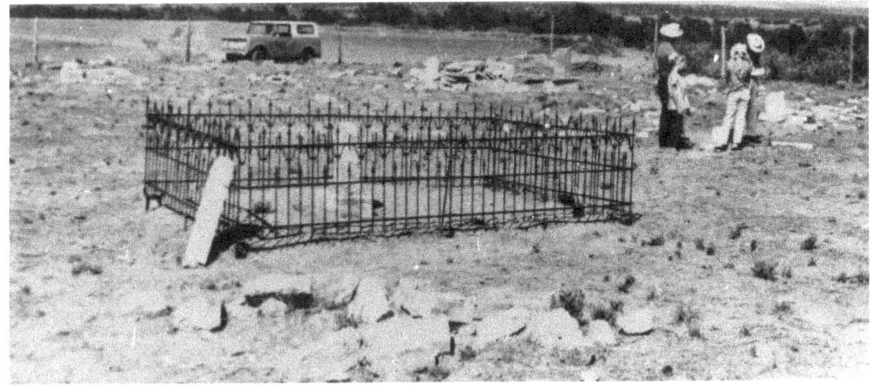

Located in Seven Rivers, the frontier cemetery was moved north to the Twin Oaks Cemetery of Artesia, New Mexico, due to the construction of Brantley Dam. *Courtesy of the Southeastern New Mexico Historical Society.*

it was written in the local newspaper that you could read the paper by the light of gunfire at night. When the graves were opened, the town's violent past became evident, as most of the graves presented bullets. Not too many citizens died of natural causes.

Dale Balzano reports that the New Mexico State Police has told him that it considers the one-mile stretch of road in front of the tiny hamlet of Seven Rivers to be one of the most haunted stretches of highway in the state. They have records of people going off the road to avoid a woman in a white dress crossing the highway, as well as other apparitions that seem to appear out of nowhere.

3

EAGLE NEST

HISTORIC EAGLE NEST

The land now known as Eagle Nest was once home to the Ute and Jicarilla Apache tribes. These peoples roamed the area in search of game and golden eagle feathers for their ritual ceremonies. When the miners arrived, Eagle Nest was being used primarily for ranching and farming

It was founded in 1919 as Therma by Talmadge "T.D." Neal, who bought the land next to the Springer brothers. Charles and Frank Springer used this land to construct a dam for the purposes of forming a lake for irrigation. As the tiny hamlet grew, residents of neighboring towns relocated there. Therma was renamed Eagle Nest when the post office was established in 1935.

One of the largest industries for Eagle Nest became the cutting and selling of ice blocks from the lake. Men were hired by T.D. Neal to travel out on the ice and cut the chunks, which were then stored in sawdust in icehouses. Many families made their living doing this in the winter months, since jobs were few and far between.

William B. Tyler was hired by Oklahoma oilman Walter Gant to begin construction on the Eagle Nest Resort in 1927. This resort was to be the finest ever built using Gant's instructions. The original Eagle Nest Lodge contained twelve rooms, a lounge and a restaurant and had fine amenities for its guests to enjoy.

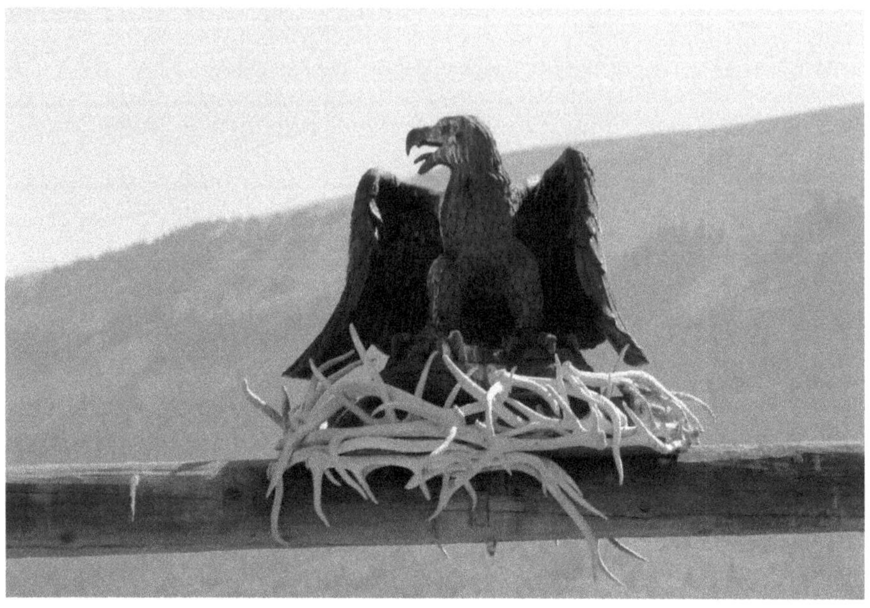

This proud bird sculpture rests in a nest of antlers on a ranch gate as the pure symbol of Eagle Nest. *Courtesy of the author.*

Located along the mountain route of the Santa Fe Trail, Eagle Nest became a good rest stop for travelers who had just ascended the steep Cimarron Canyon. Gambling was a huge draw for the village, as many visitors came to play at the roulette wheels, gaming tables and slot machines scattered throughout the town. Gaming reigned supreme until the 1940s, when a gambling crackdown began. Local history states that when the gambling halls heard of the raids, they would simply lower all the slot machines and other equipment into the lake. The few who were not quick enough witnessed their machines dragged to the middle of the streets and chopped to bits by axe-wielding police officers.

EAGLE NEST TODAY

Surrounded by the Sangre de Cristo Mountains, Eagle Nest is a picturesque community of approximately 290 souls nestled in a lovely mountain meadow known as the Moreno Valley. Eagle Nest Lake State Park, which is New Mexico's newest, will take your breath away as you top the last hill coming out of the wooded Cimarron Canyon. This large man-made lake, started in 1917, is a sports person's paradise. Among the available activities are boating, kayaking, fishing, paddle boarding, horseback riding, four-wheel-drive tours, snowboarding, rafting and hiking and bike trails.

One of the largest draws for Eagle Nest is the annual ice-fishing tournament, held the last Saturday in January. It is known to attract more than 250 hearty participants each year. Fishermen cut a hole in the thick ice crust (sometimes up to twenty-eight inches) that has formed on Eagle Nest Lake to see who will pull out the largest rainbow trout, kokanee salmon, Coho salmon, northern pike or perch. The nearly $4,000 in prize money makes enduring the sometimes minus-twenty-two-degree day worthwhile for the anglers of all ages. The tournament is proudly sponsored by the Friends Group of the Eagle Nest Lake and Cimarron Canyon State Park in cooperation with the Eagle Nest Chamber of Commerce and the New Mexico Department of Game and Fish.

Eagle Nest is also the headquarters for some of the best big- and small-game hunting in America. Trophy-sized elk, bear, mountain lion and deer can be found in the public hunt areas as well as on the private lands.

Being halfway between the state capital of Santa Fe and Raton, New Mexico, which is within miles of the Colorado border, Eagle Nest is nestled

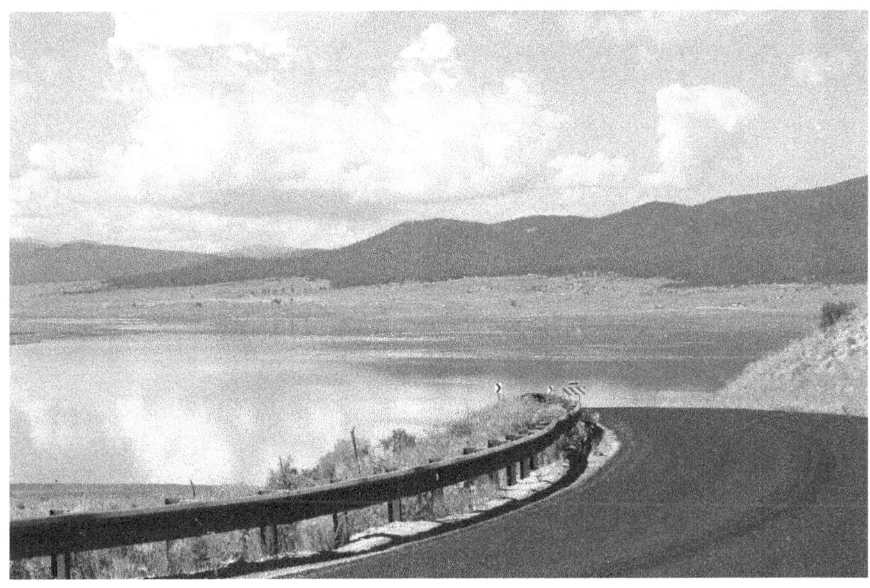

Eagle Nest Lake State Park provides visitors and residents with a multitude of activities in a gorgeous setting. *Courtesy of the author.*

in at an elevation of 8,238 feet. The town is used to copious amounts of snow (sometimes as much as 150 inches) in the winters, but it also enjoys cool, mild summers and is known as a popular vacation destination.

Eagle Nest is located at the crossroads of the Enchanted Circle Scenic Byway, the narrow road that winds lazily through some of the most spectacular scenery in New Mexico. Compliments of the Carson National Forest and the Sangre de Cristo (Blood of Christ) Mountains, the towns of Cimarron, Questa, Red River, Shady Brook, Arroyo Hondo, Angel Fire and Taos encircle the tallest mountain in New Mexico, Wheeler Peak (13,161 feet). Fall is a particularly beautiful time of the year to make the drive as the aspens turn a brilliant gold.

Although Main Street is less than one mile long, it features a wide variety of shops carrying locally made crafts, fine art, sculpture, pottery and candy, as well as T-shirts, souvenirs and Native American jewelry. The street features home-style restaurants, coffee shops and, of course, an old-time saloon complete with swinging doors.

LAGUNA VISTA LODGE

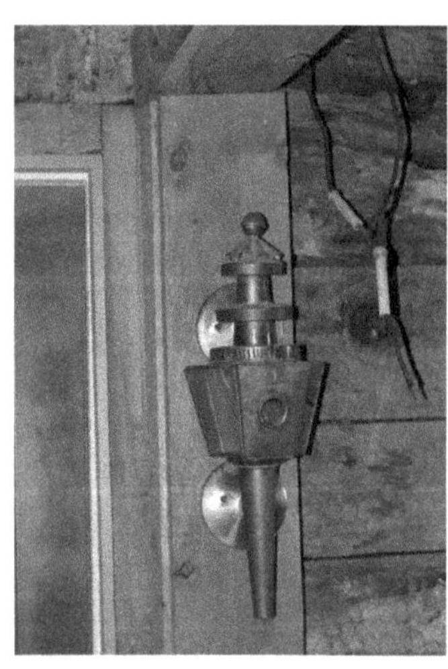

It is often said that if the pine walls of the old brothel could talk, they would have extremely interesting tales to tell. *Courtesy of the author.*

Dating back to 1897, the Laguna Vista Lodge started life as a saloon and restaurant with an upstairs brothel. The ladies of the brothel serviced the multitudes of miners who flocked to the area in search of silver and gold in the newly opened mines. If the wide-planked pine walls could talk, they would surely have a few sordid tales to tell.

Allegedly constructed of stolen railroad ties from a stockpile located in Elizabethtown five miles away, which is now a ghost town, the Laguna Vista Lodge began its life as a gambling hall, saloon and brothel called the El Monte. Some of these ties are still visible in the rooms today. It is said that locals call the lodge the "Guney."

The El Monte was said to have been frequented by politicians who stopped on

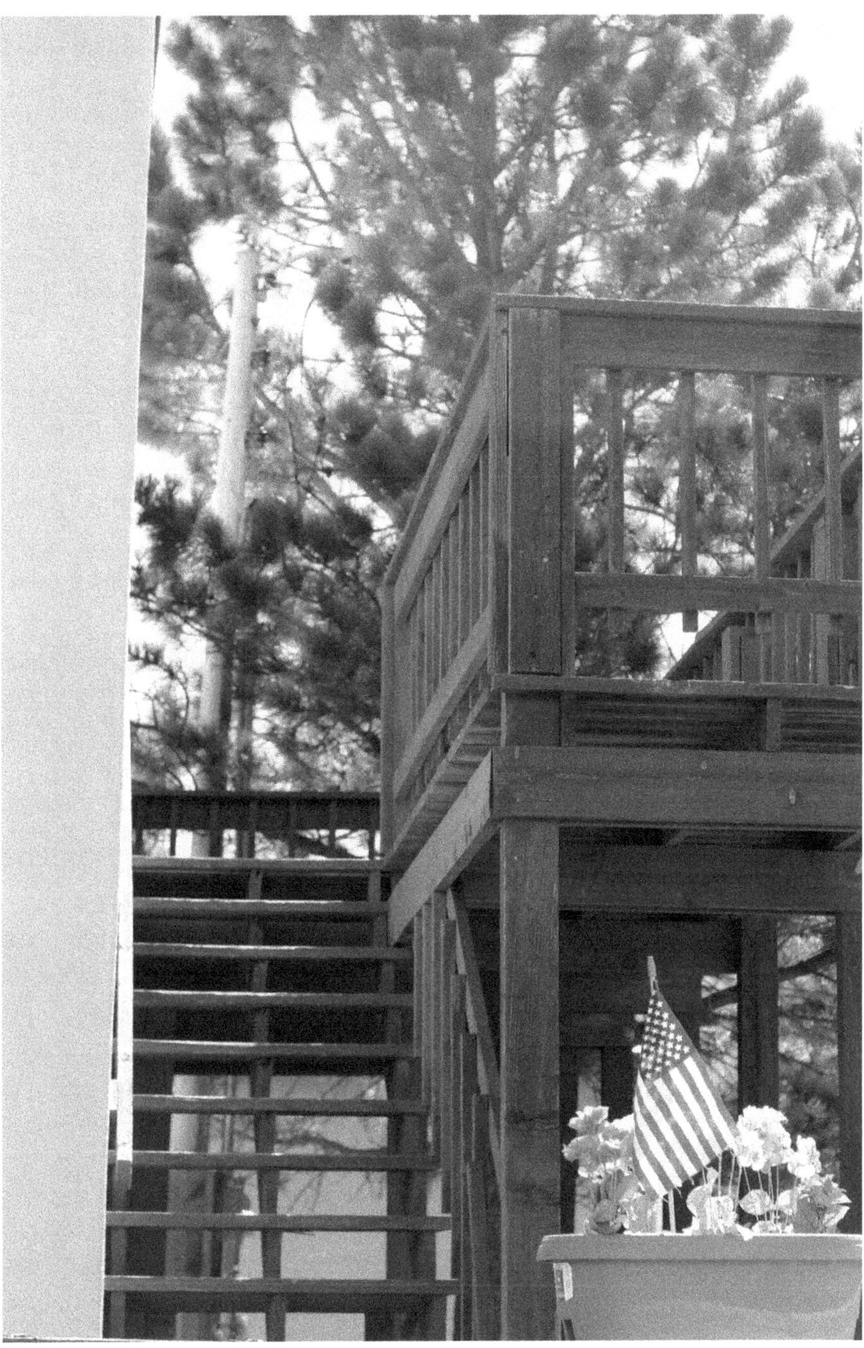

Men of high status in the community and politicians used the back staircase of the Laguna Vista Lodge to partake unnoticed in the upstairs delights. *Courtesy of the author.*

their way to the horse races in Raton, New Mexico. They were afforded their own stairway to the brothel located behind the lodge to give a sense of privacy to the gentlemen who wished to partake in the many activities of the hotel. It was the busiest saloon in the 1920s and '30s.

Owned by Gene and Pearl Wilson in the early 1900s, the El Monte was doing such great gambling business that, it is written, the Wilsons often armed themselves while transporting their gambling profits from the saloon to their living quarters to prevent being robbed. The Wilsons sold the hotel to Bob and Edith Sullivan in the early 1950s, and the Sullivans in turn built the new hotel next to the original in 1964 to accommodate the overflow.

These sordid activities were still in operation until the 1970s, when, according to local legend, a madam named Toots ran the brothel very publically until she got wind of an impending raid. Allegedly, Toots was housing underage girls in her establishment, unfortunately including her fourteen- and fifteen-year-old daughters. According to the scuttlebutt, Toots absconded from Eagle Nest in 1971 and has not been seen in the area again.

Today, only a select few can wander its halls, as a velvet rope prevents access to the "secret staircase" directly in the middle of the Calamity Jane Restaurant. Original wallpaper graces the rooms on the second floor. Another historical feature of the rooms are the genuine light fixtures, which were used to illuminate the rooms by the girls. The rooms are small, just large enough for a bed and possibly a dresser to hold the chamber pitcher. Only the most popular girls had a private sink in their rooms.

The bordello upstairs is now rented for private dining and a Miss New Mexico Saloon Girl Competition, initiated by owner Bert Clemens. This competition, held over the Labor Day weekend, "sheds light on the additional skills of the women of the Old West." The contest is not based on beauty, but on costume, creativity and charisma. It's about having fun and being entertaining.

Clemens was quoted as saying, "the tradition of the saloon and trying to preserve the Old West, that's our theme here. Back in the old days, when gambling was still prevalent, even though it was illegal, musicians would usually get up in the afternoon to play, and it would go on until the wee hours of the morning."

With New Mexico becoming a hub of movie and television activity, the Laguna Vista Lodge was a favorite gathering place for the cast of *Lonesome Dove* during filming in the region. The hotel has also been featured in *True West Magazine*, *Sunset Magazine* and on *The David Letterman Show* as well as the Travel Channel's *Resort Rescue*.

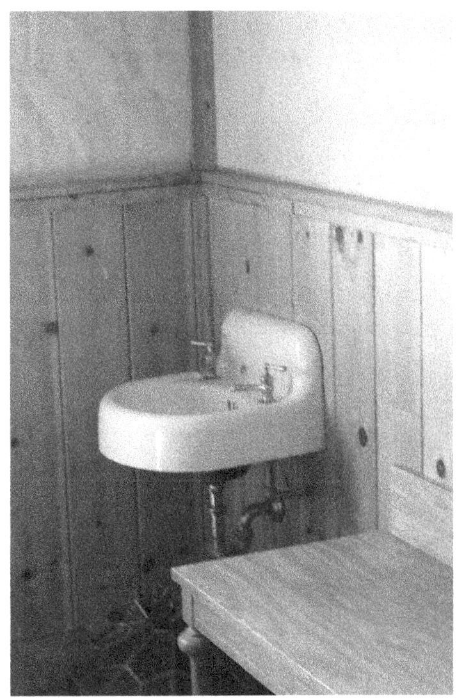

There is only one room with a sink at the brothel, so the girl who earned this luxury was highly favored among her clientele and the brothel owner. *Courtesy of the author.*

Laguna Vista Lodge has been remodeled over the years and features a beautiful honeymoon cabin complete with firepit. Several gazebos dot the property to provide guests a wonderful place in which to drink in the gorgeous vistas that surround the hotel. The lodge is proudly owned and operated by an American veteran.

Ghosts

The main spirit of the Laguna Vista Lodge is said to be named Eleanor. Her story begins normally enough—a newlywed wife on her honeymoon accompanying her husband to the area so he could go hunting. This is where Eleanor's story turns tragic. Her husband never returned to the hotel from his hunting trip, stranding her there without means. It is thought that Eleanor became a soiled dove to survive.

Eleanor's ghost supposedly remains in the old Laguna Vista Lodge and refuses to leave, awaiting her husband's return. Staff say she is harmless and has been known to haunt the dining room from time to time and startle

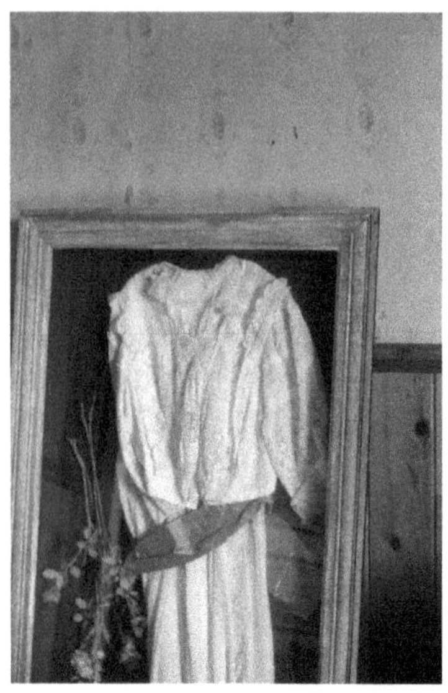

Remnant of an all-too-short-lived marriage is said to be Eleanor's wedding dress. Laguna Vista Lodge has framed this special memento in her honor. *Courtesy of the author.*

the bartender by calling her name. An elegant white dress, which could have been Eleanor's, is framed with dried roses and stands in her room as a gentle reminder of her days as a young bride.

From other accounts, Eleanor is a fan of quiet and has been known to turn off radios and to caution children not to make so much noise as they play. Sadly, it is said that Eleanor died of a broken heart by either hanging or starving herself to death.

Guests have reported trays and glasses moving on their own and vacuum cleaners turning on by themselves. Also in the kitchen is a small boy spirit known as David who was reportedly shot in the walk-in freezer area of the kitchen. He, according to investigators, is thought to constantly cry.

Bert Clemens, who bought the property in 1971 from Bob and Edith Sullivan, reports that he was told there are "at least 22 spirits lingering around the place." One apparently is musical and will play the piano while sitting on a dining room chair, while another enjoys throwing rolling pins in the restaurant kitchen. Radios without batteries have been reported to turn on by themselves on occasion.

No matter the true number of spirits supposedly contained within the walls of the Laguna Vista Hotel and Annex, investigators have not found any to be troublesome; all are harmless. The *Frommer's Travel Guide* has described the Laguna Vista Lodge as "the best restaurant and hotel in the valley."

4
Taos

Historic Taos

The Taos we know today dates to 1540, when explorer Captain Hernando Alvarado arrived with the Coronado Expedition, in search of the legendary Seven Cities of Gold, and established a small village. They thought they had found the gold they were seeking because the surface of the Taos Pueblo glistening in the sun looked like it was covered in flecks of gold. In reality, the earth of which the pueblo was made has a high content of the mineral mica, which fooled the explorers for a short time.

The name *Taos* is attributed to Don Juan de Oñate's secretary, Juan Belarde, who wrote in his journal, "this day after mass, we went on to the province of Taos which they also called Tayberon and others." The word *Tao* was credited to the Picuris Indians, whose pueblo was twenty-four miles southeast of the Taos area. They would say this word as they pointed to the northeast, where they were known to have relatives.

By 1760, the village was known as Don Fernando de Taos by the Spanish inhabitants and eventually shortened to just Taos, which means "red willow" in the native Tewa language. Also, in this year, a raid of three thousand Comanche converged on Taos Pueblo with the intent of destroying the community. The warriors took fifty-six women and children as captives, one being Maria Rosa de Villalpando, a daughter of one of the settlers who had earlier promised the child in marriage to the tribal chief. Maria refused the marriage, which angered the tribe. Maria was to live many years with the Comanche before they traded her to the Pawnee, who sold her to a Frenchman from St. Louis. She is said to have lived a long life in St. Louis with many children.

Spanish settlers begin to move to the Taos area and set up homes near the pueblo for protection. By 1821, a huge influx of Mexican immigrants began to head north along the Santa Fe Trail to the Taos area after Mexican independence from Spain.

Padre Antonio Jose Martinez, newly ordained in 1826, was assigned to the Guadalupe Parish, which included Taos. He then met Christopher Carson—better known today as Kit Carson, who, at age sixteen, had run away from Missouri. The priest baptized Kit in 1842 and performed his wedding ceremony in 1843 to Josefa Jaramillo.

TAOS TODAY

Author D.H. Lawrence was quoted as saying, "You cannot come to Taos without feeling that here is one of the chosen spots on Earth."

A quaint artist colony, one of the first established in the United States, Taos has played host to many famous artists, writers, filmmakers, musicians and actors. Art galleries—more than eighty to be exact—six world-class museums, charming restaurants and fine jewelry stores line the narrow streets that were once burro trails.

Taos also has an active music scene and features local New Mexico bands as well as acts from around the country. The city carries a certain bohemian feel, harkening back to the hippie commune days in the 1960s. Urban legend says a low-frequency hum can be heard outside of Taos proper. The source behind this hum has not been found. It is also reported that the entire valley has a magnetic quality to it—a vortex—that has succeeded in drawing so many different personalities to the region.

No doubt the picturesque landscape surrounding the village of a little more than sixty-five hundred souls has been an inspiration for those with an artistic spirit. The landmarks, setting and natural beauty of Taos have made it one of the most widely depicted towns on canvas of New Mexico. The striking views are accentuated by the adobe structures, the brightly painted windows and gates and the luscious vegetation that abounds. The clear mountain air at 6,967 feet seems to wash away troubles and concerns, leaving you relaxed and content.

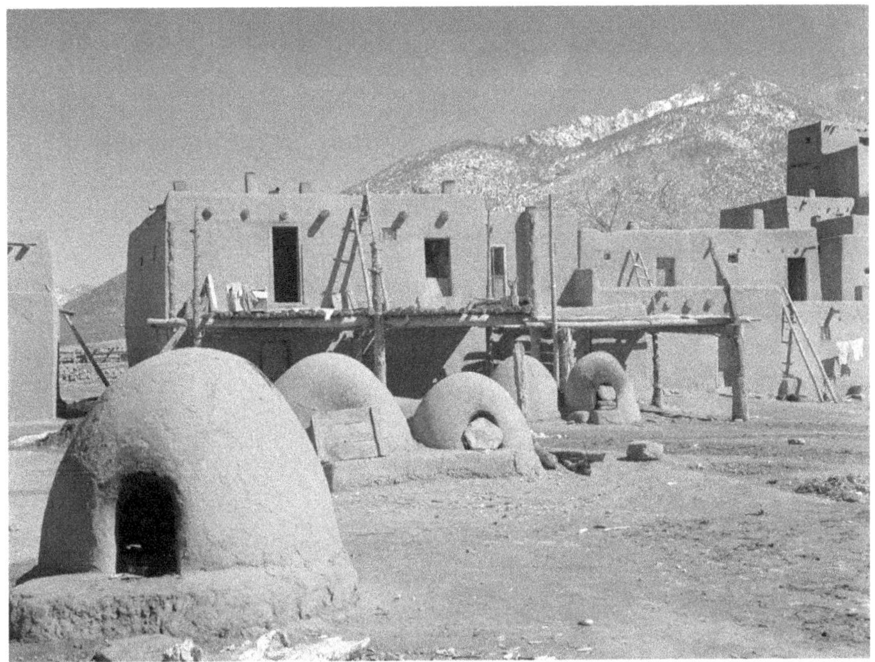

The adobe Taos Pueblo rises from the clay high desert earth as one of the distinctive landmarks in Taos. *Library of Congress.*

Although a relatively small town, Taos offers its visitors an extensive range of activities for the entire family to enjoy. The high desert terrain is perfect for hiking and mountain biking, and you cannot beat the vistas. For the more adventurous, white-water rafting is available along the Rio Grande and Embudo Rivers.

For those of you who love to hit the slopes, a ski trip to the world-class Taos Ski Valley is a must. Kachina Peak towers over the valley at an elevation of 12,481 feet and provides 150 acres of advanced slopes as well as intermediate and beginner areas.

Famous for the historical Taos Pueblo, this diverse town relies heavily on its indigenous heritage. You will find evidence of this proud culture displayed throughout Taos. Visitors from all over the world come to Taos to experience the best-preserved, still-inhabited example of ancient Puebloan culture—now a UNESCO World Heritage Site. The site helps to make Taos Pueblo one of the most visited areas in the state. Photography is not allowed at the pueblo, except by special permission, but representations of the structure can be found in many art forms.

This five-story adobe masterpiece is supported by pine log vigas with pine and aspen latillas on the ceilings, harvested from the nearby Carson National Forest. The outside is maintained every six months by applying a coat of mud, and the interiors are coated with the skim coat of thin washes of white earth. When the Taos Pueblo was first constructed, there were no doors or windows; entrance was gained from the roof by ladders for security purposes. The ladders were retracted when any signs of trouble were detected. Doors and windows were added in 1598, when the Spaniards took over the structure.

Hacienda Del Sol

As the former home of Mabel Dodge Luhan and her fourth husband, Tony Luhan, this stately property is nestled off the main Taos thoroughfare of Paseo del Pueblo, otherwise known as Highway 64, and could easily be missed if you blink. Comprised of three adobe buildings, the oldest erected in 1804, Hacienda Del Sol is situated on 1.2 acres of prime land that is also home to an estimated two thousand tulip bulbs and six hundred daffodils, which provide a fabulously colorful display when in full bloom.

Hacienda Del Sol, which means "house of the sun," was used by the Luhans as a temporary residence and as guest accommodations for their many celebrity friends who needed privacy and peace away from the rest of the world. Authors Willa Cather, D.H. Lawrence and Frank Waters, and artist Georgia O'Keeffe are but a few of the honored guests who have graced this property with their presence.

Today, the hacienda offers twelve Southwest-appointed rooms, all featuring private baths. The Southwest décor in each room honors the traditions of the region by showcasing handwoven rugs and baskets; handcrafted antique furniture; unique, original artwork; and locally stitched quilts and comforters. Some also provide a traditional kiva fireplace, private steam showers and Jacuzzi tubs. When placing your reservation, be sure to request your preference.

Many three-hundred-year-old cottonwood trees surround Hacienda Del Sol's beautifully maintained grounds, which makes a perfect venue for weddings, anniversaries and celebrations of all sorts, or just as a spot in the sun to relax and read a book as you enjoy the view of the sacred Taos Mountain. The golden willows and fragrant lilac bushes located in the courtyard exude

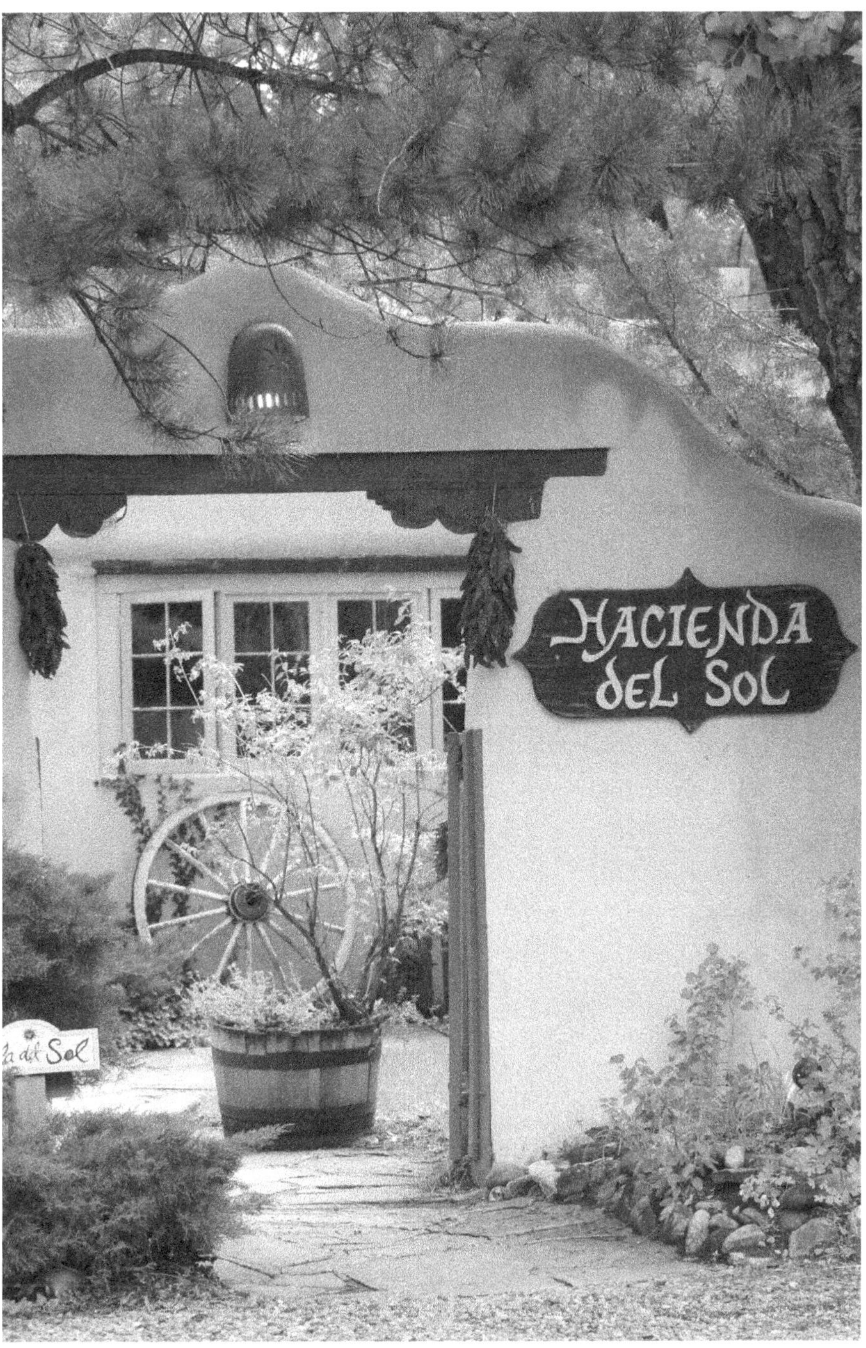

The grounds of the Hacienda Del Sol is a venue for weddings, anniversaries, birthdays or just to celebrate life, as Mabel Dodge Luhan surely did. *Courtesy of the author.*

romance, creating the perfect ambiance for a summer wedding. Later in the year, the dancing silver and gold leaves of the cottonwoods glisten like golden disks in the high desert autumn sun. Hacienda del Sol has been honored by being rated by *USA Today* as one of the ten most romantic inns in the country.

You will be pampered by the delicious made-to-order breakfast and special blended coffee provided by the innkeeper in the historic Southwest-style dining room of the main house. Snacks are also available daily. A cozy fireplace in the dining room will be sure to stave off the chill of the northern New Mexico mornings and evenings.

The resort also features private Jacuzzis and steam rooms in four rooms, as well as traditional wood-burning kiva fireplaces in four of the rooms. One room is dog friendly, so be sure to ask about the "doggie rules" when making your reservation if you are traveling with your fur baby.

Mabel Dodge Luhan, a prominent character of Taos, came to the small artist community and established several houses for herself and her many famous friends. Although quite wealthy, Luhan lived simply, many times without electricity. She was known to give away her possessions regularly. Mabel's influence can be seen throughout this Taos property.

GHOSTS

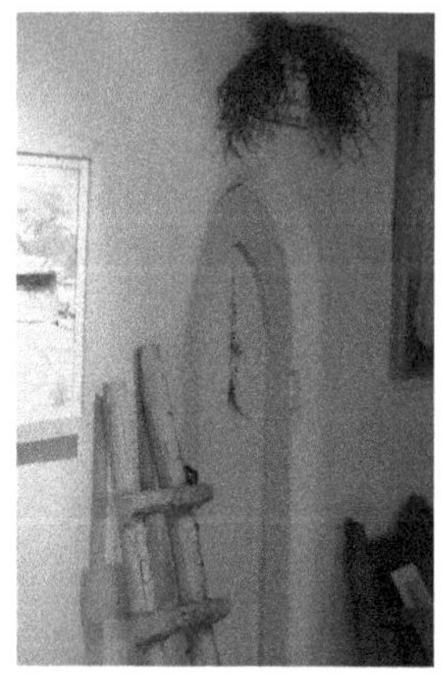

This tiny door leads to Mabel Dodge Luhan's solace, which is filled with original artwork, handwoven rugs and a kiva-style fireplace. *Courtesy of the author.*

The presence of Mabel Dodge Luhan is felt in the main part of the hacienda, especially in her room. A quaint, arched, powder-blue door offers access to the socialite's former abode. Original artworks adorn the wall, many given to Mabel as gifts from her circle of famous artist friends. Another presence felt at Hacienda Del Sol is that of Mabel's fourth husband, Tony, a native of the Taos Pueblo. Both people were larger than life on earth, so it stands to reason that they would not be very willing to leave their beloved homes.

A faint sound of drums can sometimes be heard coming from Mabel's room. As Tony was rarely without his drums, it may be safe to assume that he is serenading his wife in their cozy nest.

Owner Luellen Hertel has had guests tell her that when they put their key in the lock of Mabel's room, it is politely pushed back out, creating a startling situation for a few moments.

Another incident that Hertel talks about happened to a guest from Wisconsin, who told her she had a lengthy conversation with a man sitting by the fireplace in the dining room. During this conversation, the man asked the woman to take down certain Native American artifacts hanging around the room at the time. When shown a photograph of Tony Luhan, the guest confirmed that this indeed was the gentleman to whom she was speaking.

HISTORIC TAOS INN

The former home and office of Dr. Thomas P. Martin and his wife, Helen, the Historic Taos Inn started out as a combination of several adobe houses encircling a plaza, which now serves as the beautiful hotel lobby. Many of these dwellings were built in the 1800s, and the impressive two-and-a-half-story cupola topped with stained glass that covers the fountain in the main lobby was once the community well.

Dr. Martin, who was the only physician in the county, moved to Taos in 1890 and purchased the largest home on the plaza for his residence. Today, this structure is the Doc Martin Restaurant. The kitchen of the restaurant was the former surgical area, and the first dining area to the left, past the front desk, functioned as the birthing room.

The Historic Taos Inn now boasts a total of forty-one rooms and three suites. The owners and management strive to provide positive and lasting memories for their guests. Their brochure states, "The Inn was founded on a rich legacy of excellence. Our guests are eager to sample the atmosphere of old Taos yet expect modern amenities. So our goal is to deliver just that. We aim to provide the finest personal services in warm, relaxed surroundings."

As you step through the arched, bright-blue front door and past the thick adobe walls, you will feel transported into a different realm, one that once saw the following celebrities lounging in the lobby: actress Greta Garbo, Wild West show performer Pawnee Bill and famed author D.H. Lawrence, who was known to frequent many of the establishments in Taos as a close friend of Georgia O'Keeffe and socialite Mabel Dodge Luhan. It is reported that, more recently, actors Robert Redford and Jessica Lange have been seen

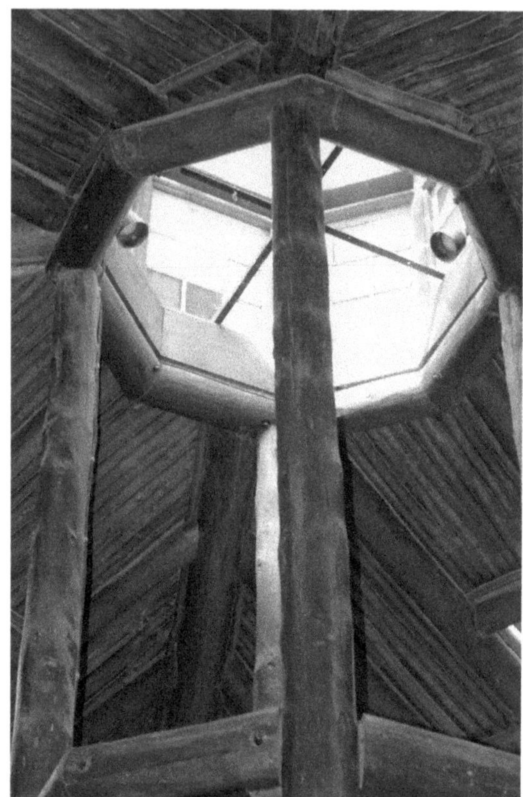

Left: Interior cupola in the lobby of Taos Inn was a water well for the entire village. It is incorporated as a striking feature. *Courtesy of the author.*

Below: This tiny nook with street views just inside Doc Martin's Restaurant was once a birthing room in the namesake's clinic. *Courtesy of the author.*

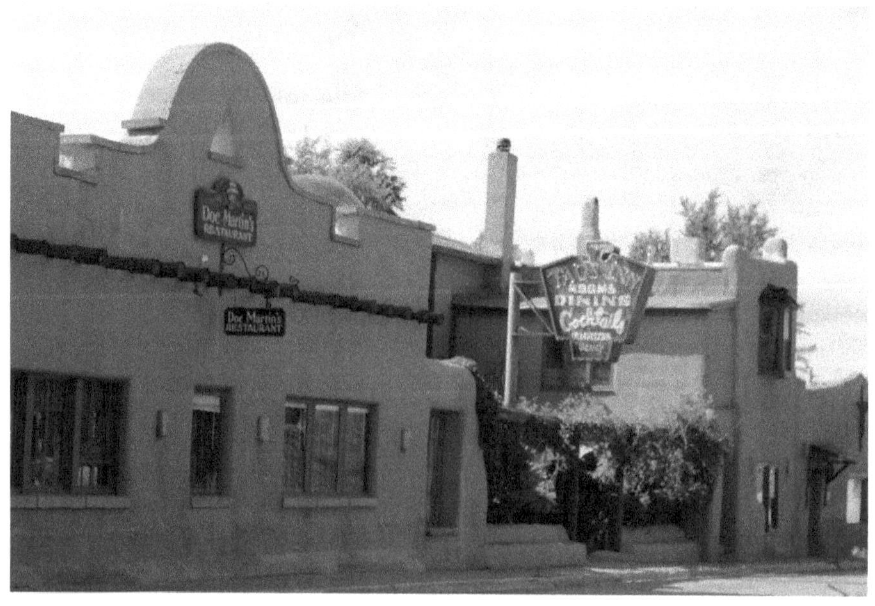

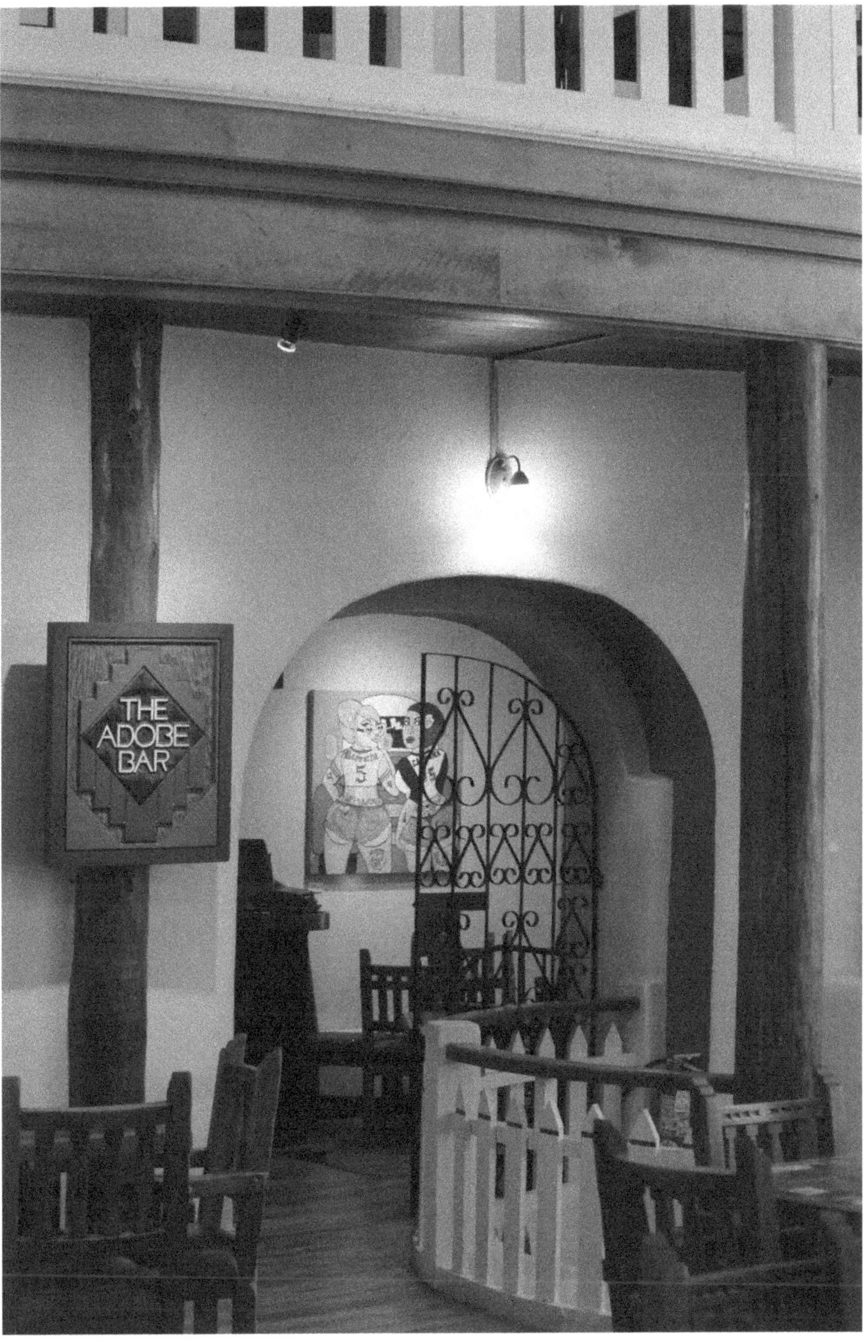

The Adobe Bar, the place to see and be seen in Taos. The bar is frequented by many celebrities during their visits to New Mexico. *Courtesy of the author.*

enjoying one of the celebrated margaritas of the Adobe Bar in the Historic Taos Inn lobby.

Although a person who liked to keep to himself, Martin went out of his way to make sure his patients received the very best of care, no matter the terrain. For this reason, he was highly respected, becoming a celebrity in his own right.

For those of you who enjoy art history, this piece of trivia will be of interest: the world-renowned Taos Society of Artists—or the "Taos Six"—whose members were Joseph Henry Sharp, Ernest Blumenschein, Bert Phillips, Oscar E. Berninghaus, W. Herbert Dunton and E. Irving Couse, was started in the dining room of the Martin house in 1912. Phillips, Helen Martin's brother-in-law, was one of the founding members of the society, along with Blumenschein. The society prompted the Martins to acquire the rest of the surrounding properties and rent them out to visiting artists and writers.

GHOSTS

Several spirits have claimed the Historic Taos Inn for their own. One of the most famous stems from a rather gruesome event that occurred in a tiny outbuilding that was absorbed by the inn. The murder of Arthur Manby caused quite a stir in the close-knit community and still is unsolved. Manby, known as the most hated man in Taos because of his swindling, lived just off the premises at the time of his death.

Manby was ruthless in getting what he wanted and would stop at nothing to accomplish his goals—even if this included extortions or murder. His ways caught up with him, and he himself was murdered on July 1, 1929, by decapitation. It was written that his head was so badly mangled by his two dogs in the home that he was not recognizable. This led to rumors that it was not actually Manby, that he had murdered someone else, so he could escape to Europe. Nothing was ever proven.

His room, number 109, is now part of the Historic Taos Inn property and is rented upon request. A figure of a man who fits Manby's description is seen standing by the fireplace on occasion. In addition, cold temperatures are felt in the room by the housekeeping staff.

Doc Martin's restaurant kitchen, which shares a common wall with Arthur Manby's former home, sees some unusual activity from time to time in the form of pots, pans and kitchen appliances flying off the counters

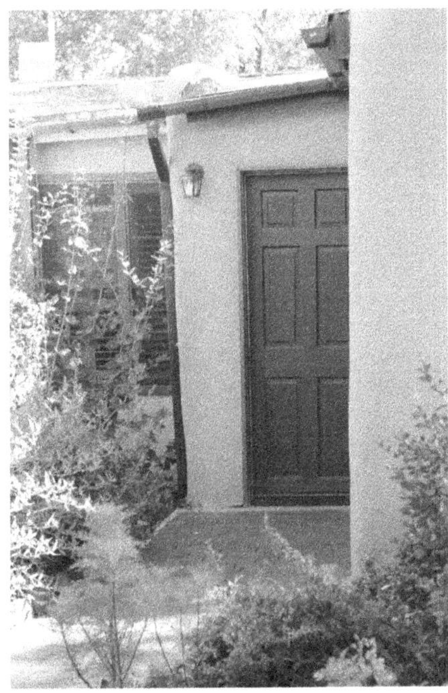

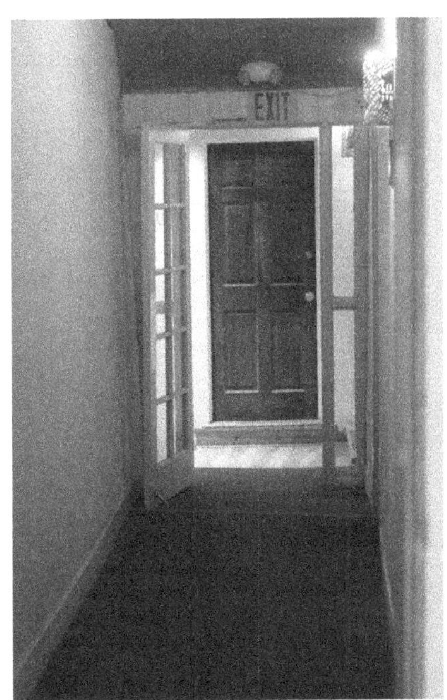

Left: The door to Arthur Manby's room is pleasant and shows none of the horrors that occurred inside in 1929. His presence is still felt here. *Courtesy of the author.*

Right: The Historic Taos Inn's hallway is said to be traveled by more than just hotel guests from time to time. A cowboy finds this enjoyable, too. *Courtesy of the author.*

and landing on the floor without any human impetus. Reports of doors opening and closing on their own and lights flashing in the dining room are commonplace.

Rumor has it that a cowboy, complete with jangling spurs, wanders the halls of the main lobby area and has made his presence known to a select, lucky few. He has also been known to visit certain rooms just to say hello.

Room 102 is known to have the faint smell of roses. The figure of a tall woman has been seen in the doorway to room 106. The woman appears to exit the room through a mirror that is left crooked after her departure. Room 206 had figures painted on the fireplace. After several guests left suddenly, the fireplace was repainted, and the problem seems to have been fixed.

The Adobe Bar allegedly has an apparition that likes to call out the staff's names when they are alone after closing.

5
SANTA FE

HISTORIC SANTA FE

Often referred to as the "City Different," Santa Fe lives up to its name. As the oldest capital city in the United States, founded in 1610 by Spanish colonists, Santa Fe has seen many changes and upheavals. Santa Fe ("holy faith") began its existence with a grand name. La Villa Real de la Santa Fe de San Francisco de Asís is its official name ("The Royal City of the Holy Faith of Saint Francis of Assisi"). St. Francis Cathedral is a tribute to this gentle saint as well.

As the fourth-largest city in New Mexico, Santa Fe has always been an economic hub. The early Tewa people built their villages several hundred years before the insurgence of the Spaniards in this area. They called their settlement Ogha Po'oge, which means "white shell water place." They were followed by the Tanoans and Puebloan people, who established pueblo structures in the area close to the Santa Fe River.

Most of northern New Mexico was involved in the Revolt of 1680, also known as Popè's Rebellion, when the native people revolted against the Spaniard inhabitants. The result was the deaths of more than four hundred Spanish men, women and children, as well as the complete exile of two thousand colonists, who were able to escape from the lands the Spaniards had taken from the Puebloan people. An attempt by the native people to wipe out all existence of the Spanish culture was then complete. During

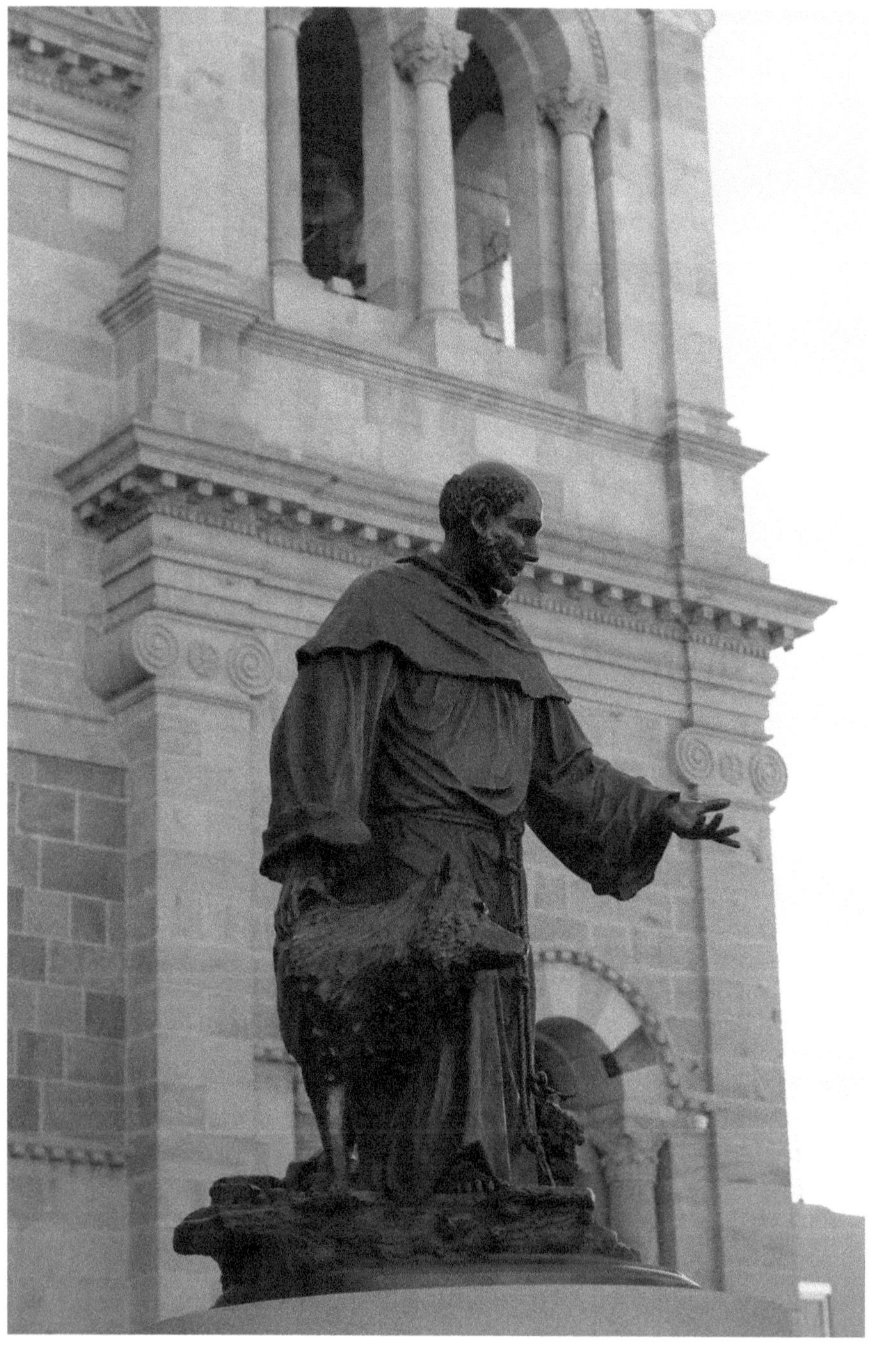

St. Francis Cathedral was built at the request of Bishop Jean-Baptiste Lamy, who is immortalized in statue form in front of his beloved church. *Courtesy of the author.*

this cleanse, many manuscripts, churches and works of art were destroyed. This happened in all the surrounding towns and villages, including Taos and Albuquerque.

The revolt was an ingenious plan devised by Popè, a medicine man from San Juan who demanded absolute secrecy from his people. He developed a message system involving a knotted rope that was taken by messenger to the pueblos without the knowledge of their oppressors. Each knot represented a day and time, so each of the pueblos were aware of when to commence its attacks.

The main reason for the revolt stemmed from the Spaniards' demand that the native people abandon all their religious beliefs and convert to Catholicism. The penalty for not complying was imprisonment and death. In 1675, forty-seven medicine men were arrested from the pueblos and tried for witchcraft. Four of these men were found guilty and hanged. This sparked even more hatred for the Spaniards among the Pueblo people and was the impetus for initiation of the plan.

Once the revolt was over, the native people returned to their everyday lives and did not continue the fight. Slowly, by 1692, the Spaniards had returned and reestablished their colonies, but because the ancient Pueblo people had proven their point and gained the respect of the Spanish, they were able to maintain their traditions and rituals without punishment.

The city as we know it today was created by New Mexico's second Spanish governor, Don Pedro de Peralta, at the foot of the magnificent Sangre de Cristo ("blood of Christ") Mountain range. Santa Fe would remain under Spanish rule until 1824, when it became the capital of the Mexican territory. The city would then be claimed by the Republic of Texas once it seceded from Mexico in 1836. In 1846, Brigadier General Stephen W. Kearny and 1,700 of his soldiers conquered Santa Fe to obtain it and the entire New Mexico Territory for the United States. This status was made official by the signing of the Treaty of Guadalupe Hidalgo in 1848.

Santa Fe Today

Modern-day Santa Fe has become a mecca for celebrities and those who seek a break from the surrounding world. One whiff of the piñon-scented air on a cool fall evening will grab your soul. Whether you are strolling along the famous art avenue, Canyon Road or experiencing the Santa Fe Plaza with the Native American vendors selling their beautiful handmade items, you will surely see something new and exciting at every glance.

Santa Fe is truly a visually beautiful city. The vivid southwestern colors, foliage, brightly painted doors, gorgeous mountain backdrop and adobe architecture will lure you into the quaint shops and restaurants and transport you back in time. Many of the shops surrounding the Santa Fe Plaza are original structures of the 1600s and later, with only a small number of upgrades. According to city ordinance, all structures built in and around the historic district must adhere to the Pueblo or Territorial styles of architecture.

A unique venue has popped up in recent years and is causing quite a stir. The Meow Wolf is a place where all the hip people hang out. Musical acts from all over come to the setting to be seen and heard. It is the epitome of the "City Different" vibe. Called the "House of Eternal Return," Meow Wolf is a Victorian house built inside a former bowling alley. Owned by local author George R.R. Martin, of *Game of Thornes* fame, the Meow Wolf is accessed through fireplaces, refrigerators and other one-of-a-kind portals.

For ski buffs, Ski Santa Fe provides a challenging experience at the top of Mount Baldy, which rises 10,350 feet above the town. Santa Fe sees approximately 225 inches of snow per year, which feeds the eighty-three trails in the 660-acre basin. Billed as "one of the country's most diverse and unique ski destinations" by the New Mexico Ski Hall of Fame, Ski Santa Fe was started by famed thrill-seeker and New Mexico Ski Hall of Fame inductee Ben Abruzzo and his business partner, Bob Nordhaus, in 1984. The Abruzzo family still runs the resort today.

The Santa Fe Plaza and surrounding blocks provide visitors with access to art galleries, high-end jewelry shops, Christmas shops, international shops, a variety of clothing and kitchenware stores, museums, a library, nostalgic stores, as well as a multitude of restaurants and bistros. One of the largest draws to the Santa Fe Plaza is the handmade native jewelry for sale under the veranda of the Palace of the Governors. All of the items sold under the Portal (front porch) at the Governors Palace must adhere to strict rules put in place in 1936 by the Native American Vendors Program, which was developed by the Museum of New Mexico. The rules of the program state that all of the items presented by vendors for sale under this popular portal must be handcrafted by native people and authentic in order to be sold to the more than 2.4 million visitors to the Santa Fe Plaza location each year.

LA POSADA DE SANTA FE RESORT AND SPA

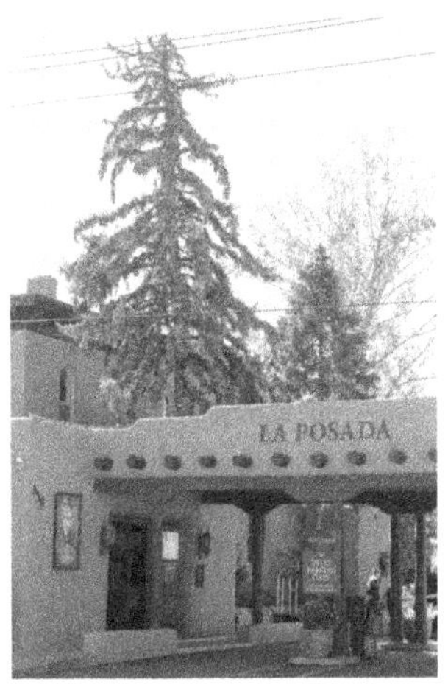

Nestled just two blocks east of the Santa Fe Plaza is La Posada de Santa Fe Resort. The name means "inn" or "resting place." *Courtesy of the author.*

Billed as one of the most renowned resorts in Santa Fe, La Posada de Santa Fe is a distinctly beautiful hotel offering many high-end amenities. Sitting on six acres of prime Santa Fe real estate, La Posada has the privilege of being the only resort located in downtown Santa Fe.

The original structure, situated on Palace Avenue, was a three-story Second Empire–style mansion and carriage house built in 1882 by wealthy Santa Fe merchant Abraham Staab and his wife, Julia. This home played host to many of Santa Fe's elite in elaborate events, which Julia would extend to her family and friends. This home was appointed with many European fineries not easily found in the wilds of the New Mexico Territory.

The Staab House is now the bar of La Posada de Santa Fe Resort and Spa; in the 1930s, owners R.H. and Eulalia Nason built a series of Pueblo-style casitas around the existing Staab Mansion and carriage house. The Nasons were to name their business La Posada, which means "inn" or "place of rest." They opened a summer arts school, which became a significant part of the Santa Fe art culture and attracted many well-known artists.

Additional construction of lodging areas and massive renovations in the 1990s produced the magnificent La Posada de Santa Fe Resort and Spa we have today. Today, the resort celebrates the life of the "lady of the house," Julia Staab, in the form of Julia's Spirited Restaurant and Bar, named in her honor.

GHOSTS

Socialite Julia Staab loved her home so much that, it is said, she never left. But that was not always the case. Her spirit has been described as a gentle ghost.

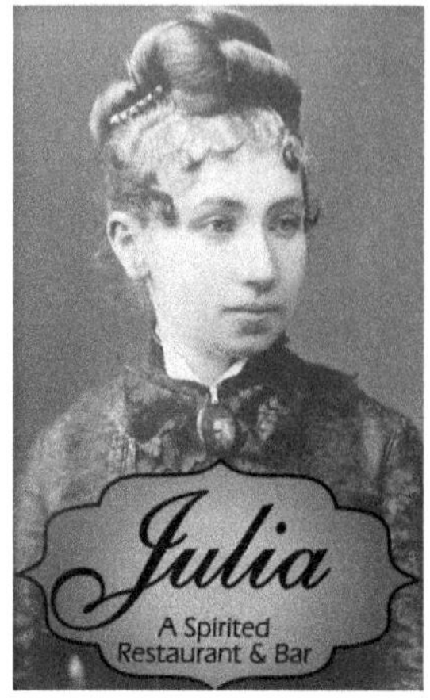

Julia Staab is said to have loved her home so much, she is still there, seen walking down the original staircase of her beautiful house. *Courtesy of the author.*

As a young woman, Julia Schuster grew up in Lügde, Germany, in the same town as her future husband, Abraham Staab. Abraham came to America at age fifteen to join his brother Zadoc to work for their cousins the Spiegelbergs in Santa Fe. The brothers opened a dry goods store in 1859 on the Santa Fe Plaza. By 1865, Abraham had made enough money to return to Germany and marry Julia on Christmas Day. When the couple returned to Santa Fe, Julia was shocked at the lack of amenities in their humble home on Burro Alley.

The couple would have seven children and, by all accounts, was a happy couple, until the death of their eighth child, a daughter. Julia reportedly became severely depressed and often fell ill and returned to Germany frequently for spa treatments, sometimes accompanied by two of her daughters, Delia and Bertha. It is through Bertha's diary entries that her great-granddaughter, Hannah Nordhaus, would become interested in her family history and pen the book *American Ghost: The True Story of a Family's Haunted Past.*

Written accounts state that Julia's light brown hair became white overnight due to the death of her child and that her sanity was often questioned. Julia tried unsuccessfully to conceive another child, which led to multiple miscarriages. Secluding herself in her room, Julia eventually died at age fifty-two in 1896, in that room. Many questions still swirl around her death. Was it suicide? Was it murder? Was Abraham having an affair? Did he kill his wife?

According to Nordhaus, her family story was one of "sadness, madness and forbidden love, drug addiction, suicide, knives to the bosom, disinheritance, lawsuits and family feuds." But despite the rumors about Julia, she was still a remarkable woman who accomplished much in her brief time on earth.

The presence of Julia is most often seen garbed in black and standing at the top of the staircase, which was once the front steps to her mansion. This staircase, framed by the original heavy hand-carved wooden doors, now leads to the guest rooms upstairs. She has also been seen sitting quietly on a chair in the bar, weeping. Other accounts have her sending bar glasses and ladies' makeup flying.

Other sightings come from guests who have stayed in Julia's room and reported the bathwater running in the middle of the night. (Julia loved baths.) The first reported encounter with Julia came in 1970, when the hotel's furnace stopped working. When workers tried to enter the furnace room, it was locked, and they could not gain access. A call was received at the front desk from an unoccupied Julia's room; a woman's voice stated, "This is my house, why isn't the furnace working? I'll get it fixed." The front desk reported that within ten minutes the furnace was indeed working, and the door was unlocked.

Besides Julia, another spirit of an old Native American man resides in La Posada de Santa Fe Resort and Spa. He is said to have died in 1096.

La Fonda on the Plaza Santa Fe

Present-day La Fonda on the Plaza Santa Fe stands on the site of Santa Fe's first inn, which was built in 1607. This fact makes the property the "oldest hotel corner in America," according to the La Fonda's four-hundred-year published history, which can be found under the "Our History" tab on the inn's website. Located directly at the start of the Santa Fe Trail and the end of the Camino Real, La Fonda on the Plaza and its predecessors provided lodging and food to the many travelers who were either on their way west to the goldfields or east to more civilized surroundings.

History states soon after 1821, Captain William Becknell successfully completed a trading expedition from Missouri to Santa Fe, ushering in the official opening of the Santa Fe Trail. In 1846, after the American conquest, La Fonda on the Plaza was the only real hotel in town and would see many name and owner changes. The first American Anglo woman to travel the Santa Fe Trail, Mary Donoho, and her husband, William, owned a hotel on this site known as La Fonda (which means inn) Americana from 1833 to 1837.

Other names, including the Santa Fe House, the U.S. Hotel and the Exchange Hotel (owned by Abraham Staab of La Posada de Santa Fe Resort and Spa), as well as many others, graced the hotel before it became La Fonda on the Plaza. Despite the valiant efforts of Staab and the community, the Exchange Hotel became derelict and had to be razed in 1919. According to Sandra D. Lynn in her book *Windows on the Past: Historic Lodging of New Mexico*, Staab devised a patriotic plan: for every $100 war bond sold, a tank nicknamed the Mud Puppy would bash against the adobe walls. It did not take long before the Exchange Hotel was just a mention in history.

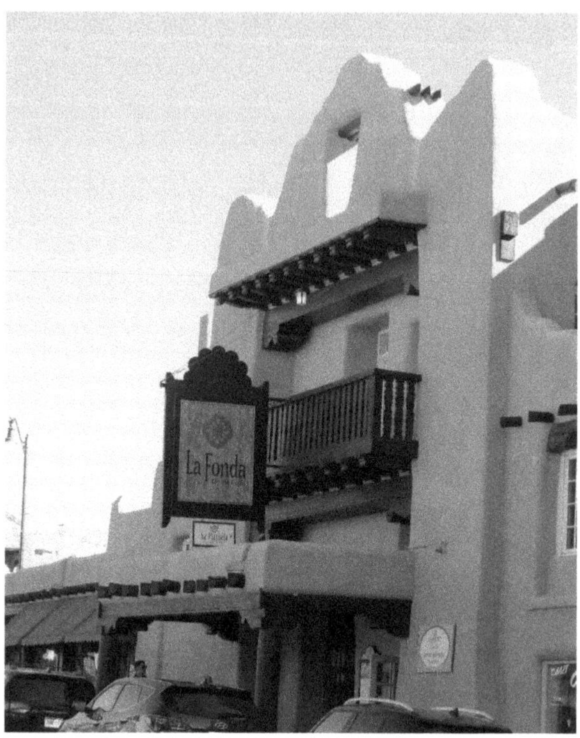

La Fonda on the Plaza is a distinctive landmark across from the St. Francis Cathedral in the heart of Santa Fe. *Courtesy of the author.*

Santa Fe's loyal citizens rallied around the idea of having one of the finest hotels in the West built in the City Different, and they raised $200,000 to finance this dream.

The magnificent adobe structure we are familiar with today was built in 1922 with the design inspirations of John Gaw Meem and Mary Coulter. These conceptions include the cathedral ceilings reaching twenty-five feet, intricately carved wooden beams, hammered tin chandeliers, terra-cotta tiles and—most impressive—the stained-glass skylights. La Fonda on the Plaza takes up an entire city block in the heart of the capital city and is a stone's throw from the famed Cathedral Basilica of St. Francis of Assisi.

A longtime landmark, La Fonda on the Plaza has taken many smaller businesses under its wing and provided Santa Fe and its hundreds of thousands of visitors a wonderful place to enjoy French pastries, unique gift shops, world-class art galleries, exclusive jewelry stores and exquisite clothing shops.

By 1925, La Fonda on the Plaza was turned into a Harvey House by founder Fred Harvey, who leased the property to serve as one of his hospitality houses along the Atchison, Topeka & Santa Fe Railway lines. To

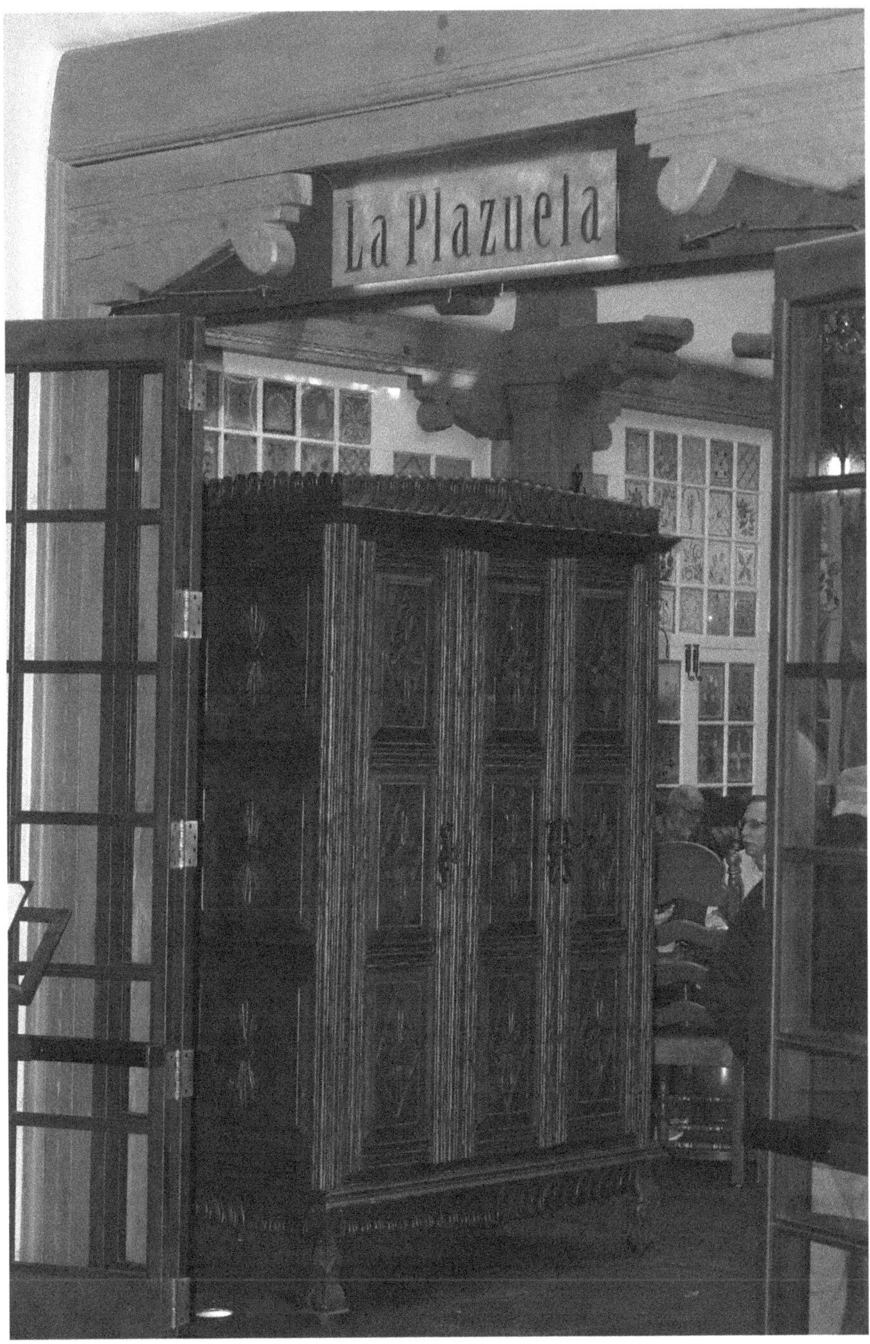

La Fonda on the Plaza's dining room, La Plazuela, is one of the most active sites on the property for reports of apparitions. *Courtesy of the author.*

entice tourists, this Harvey House would bring in Native Americans to set up in their unique Demonstration Room within the hotel, to show how they did the fine silversmithing and exquisite rug weaving that were trademarks of the local tribes. Ahead of his time, Fred Harvey would provide tours into tribal lands and show the importance of the native art form to visitors.

Among the dignitaries and celebrities who have stayed at La Fonda on the Plaza are actors Errol Flynn and Olivia de Havilland, aviator Charles Lindbergh, author Willa Cather, artist Willard Clark and U.S. presidents Rutherford Hayes, Ulysses S. Grant, John F. Kennedy and Bill Clinton. These are but a few of the names that can be dropped in connection to La Fonda on the Plaza.

The hotel would remain a Harvey House until 1968, when it was acquired by Sam and Ethel Ballen, who were lucky enough to own it until 2014 and invested millions of dollars into the project. It was then that La Fonda on the Plaza passed to the private hands of Jennifer Kimball and her brother Philip Wise (with his business firm Cienda Partners), who were longtime friends of the Ballens.

Considered a true national treasure and the epitome of Santa Fe style, La Fonda on the Plaza retains its unique character and fascinating history for the many generations to come and is proud to be a member of Historic Hotels of America, from which it received the 2016 award for Best Historic Hotel (76–200 rooms).

La Fonda on the Plaza is the perfect enchanted venue for a magical wedding, a business conference, a grand banquet or just to be pampered in the world-class spa. Be sure to check out the Bell Tower Bar atop the historic adobe, where you will be able to sip your favorite cocktail while viewing one of New Mexico's legendary sunsets.

GHOSTS

As with any hotel sporting a four-hundred-year history, rumors of spirits abound, none of which have been debunked or proven, so use your own discretion. La Fonda on the Plaza is not the source of these stories; these tales have been passed down primarily by word of mouth.

In 1862, a Texas cowboy began to shoot up La Fonda in revenge for a friend and shot a lawyer in the stomach and another man in the arm during the fracas. The cowboy was lynched in the backyard of the hotel.

His shadow hanging from the tree is reportedly seen when the light is right on the patio.

One ghost story involves a murder. On December 15, 1867, the chief justice of the Territorial New Mexico Supreme Court, John P. Slough, was shot and killed during a violent disagreement with a member of the House of Representatives of the Territorial Legislature from Doña Ana County, W.L. Rynerson (who was also the personal attorney of Charles B. Eddy, of Carlsbad), whom Slough had called a liar and a thief. New Mexico was an unruly territory, and many disagreements were settled at the end of a pistol. Rynerson was tried and acquitted on the ever-popular self-defense plea. It is rumored that Judge Slough's spirit still roams the halls and lobby of the La Fonda.

Another popular rumor dates to the inception of the inn where the La Fonda now resides. It states that the first inn was also a place where court was held, and the prisoners who were found guilty were hanged in the lobby. Spirits of these poor souls are said to still be present on the site.

A deep well was in the center of the La Fonda's dining room, now known as La Plazuela. Legend has it that a traveling salesman leapt to his death in

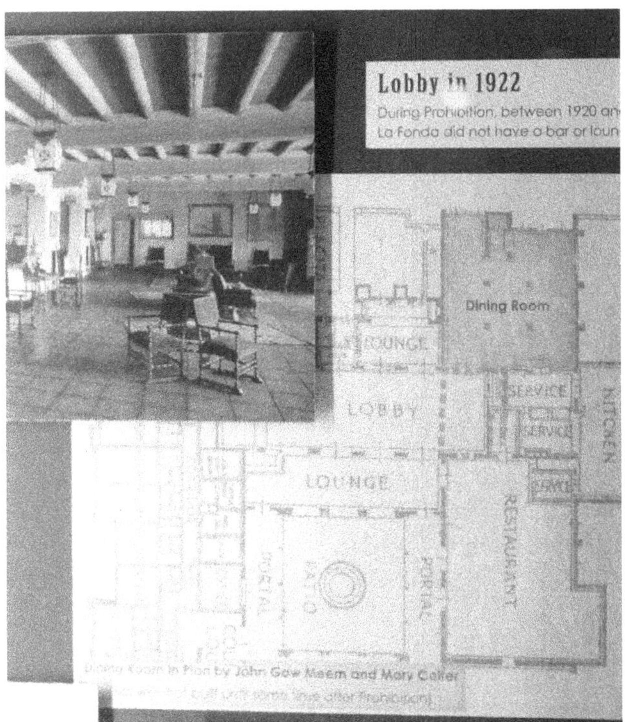

A drawing of the La Fonda lobby hangs in a side hall of the hotel and gives visitors an insight to the original structural form. *Courtesy of the author.*

the well after losing all his company's money in a card game. An apparition of a man who appears to walk to the center of the dining room, jump and then disappear has been reported by the staff over the years. Nothing was written about this incident in the local newspapers at the time; the first written report was in 1991.

Room 510—the Honeymoon Suite—is supposedly haunted by a young bride who was murdered by her former lover. Another story also exists about this couple. It states that the newly married couple checked into the hotel in the 1930s, and the husband began drinking heavily at the bar, got into an argument with the bartender and was shot dead at the bottom of the steps going to their room. The bride found her dead husband and pulled out a Derringer and shot herself. No reports were published in local newspapers of this incident.

6

CIMARRON

Historic Cimarron

Its name literally translates as "wild and unruly." Cimarron was the epitome of a Wild West town. Close enough to the mountains and mining leases, Cimarron was the hub of the area and is steeped with history. Once home to several native tribes such as the Ute, Anasazi and Jicarilla Apache and part of the highly disputed Maxwell Land Grant, Cimarron became the center of the region as gold and silver miners, cowboys and businessmen came to the well-named mountain community to seek their fortunes.

A young fur trapper by the name of Lucien Bonaparte Maxwell wandered onto the Beaubien-Miranda Ranch in northern New Mexico, where he met and married Luz Beaubien, one of the rancher's six daughters. Eventually, Lucien was fortunate enough to inherit the ranch and in 1858 built a mansion on the site where the town of Cimarron stands today.

Cimarron is on the Cimarron River, a tributary of the Canadian River, which begins farther north at the Eagle Nest Dam. Ranching is as much a vital part of the livelihood of the region today as it was in the 1800s and is what saved the town from extinction due to the railroad passing it by. Cimarron was officially chartered in 1859 and became the county seat of Colfax County in 1872 as a mere stage stop along the Mountain Branch of the Santa Fe Trail.

Because the Atchison, Topeka & Santa Fe Railway chose to run through nearby Springer, New Mexico, the county seat was moved there in 1881. In 1905, another rail company, the St. Louis, Rocky Mountain and Pacific Railway Company, laid tracks from Raton, New Mexico, to Ute Park (which lies between Cimarron and Eagle Nest) to haul coal. The railway was utilized heavily by freight and passengers until the tracks were removed during World War II to help with the war efforts.

Logging and coal mining played a huge part in forming the town we are familiar with today. Local Douglas fir and ponderosa pine were cut and made into support beams for the local mines and were also used as construction materials for many of the buildings in Cimarron and surrounding towns.

CIMARRON TODAY

The quaint mountain village today caters to curious tourists who come to the beautiful setting to soak in the mountain views, shop the many unique storefronts in both the old and new town plazas and partake in the variety of activities provided by the surrounding mountains. Hiking, fishing, biking and camping are the most popular pastimes.

Historic Cimarron provides a walking tour of the old downtown area, including the Express St. James Hotel, the original jail, a stage office and the Old Aztec Mill Museum. During this tour, you will learn about the wild history of the town, its beginnings as part of the Maxwell Land Grant (encompassing 1,713,000 acres), as well as the fifteen-year range war known as the Colfax County War. The Cimarron Chamber of Commerce states that its quaint town is "where the West is still wild."

As home to the Philmont Boy Scout Camp, which sits four miles south of the town, Cimarron became the largest campsite in America. Thousands of Boy Scouts, parents and leaders descend upon the small town several times each year to participate in jamborees and camps. Nature is a wonderful classroom and provides an excellent setting for those working on their badges or toward Eagle Scout status. Local businesses cater to the Boy Scouts and their needs.

The Villa Philmonte, on the grounds of the Philmont Boy Scout Camp, was the summer home of Oklahoma oilman Waite and his wife, Genevieve Phillips, who completed building the Spanish Mediterranean home in 1927. Described as a "mansion in the wilderness," the villa has fifteen major rooms

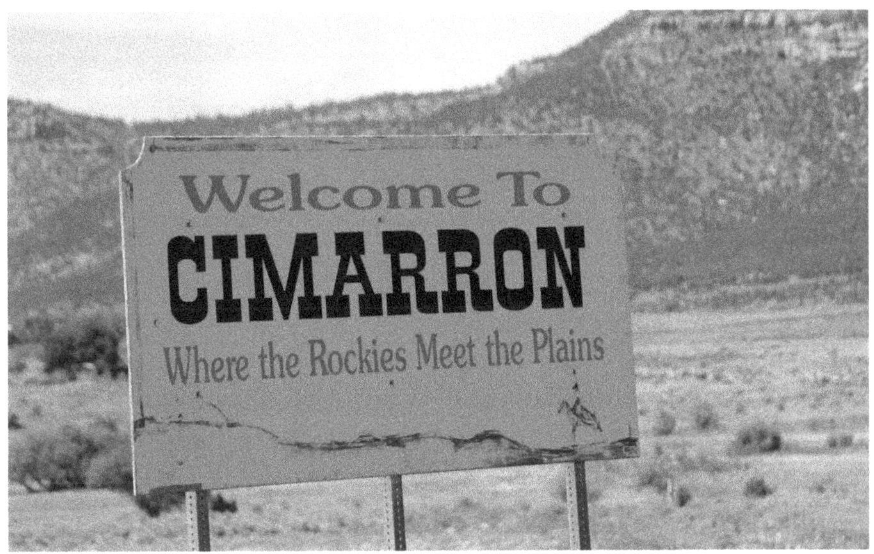

Cimarron greets visitors with a sign just outside of town that reminds them it is where the Rockies meet the Plains. *Courtesy of the author.*

and five bathrooms. The camp is a large source of employment for the region, especially Cimarron. Some locals report that the camp is 70 percent of their business each year. Phillips gifted this magnificent ranch to the Boy Scouts of America in 1941. He included the mansion as well as more than 127,000 acres of some of the most beautiful land in America.

Urraca Mesa, located within the boundaries of the Philmont Boy Scout Camp, is also a source of strange activity. Known to hold the record as the mountain most often struck by lightning per year in the state, the mesa also is the subject of Navajo legends. The Navajos believe that the mountain is the gate to hell and the site of a great battle between humans and the dark forces of evil. The word *urraca* means "magpie"; according to native legend, if a magpie calls your name, you will die soon. Due to the high iron and lodestone content of the mesa, compasses do not work correctly in the area. People hiking in the area have reported strange occurrences such as hearing voices, having odd animals following them, and getting the sensation that someone is watching them always.

A drive down the narrow two-lane highway through Cimarron Canyon will leave you breathless as you pass the magnificent towering Palisades. Here, you can get out of your vehicle, take photographs or do some fly-fishing while you enjoy the crisp, clear mountain air. Although rare encounters have happened, campers are always cautioned to be aware of the large bear population in the area.

Cimarron is surrounded by many famous ranches, such as the Chase Ranch, Ted Turner's Vermejo Park Ranch (also known as the Ladder Ranch)—which has a large population of American bison and Bolson tortoises—and the CS Ranch. There is also country singer R.W. Hampton's Clearview Ranch and the Express UU Bar Ranch, which was formerly owned by Waite Phillips. The Express St. James Hotel is also a holding of the Express UU Bar Ranch.

If it is outdoor adventure you seek, Cimarron is the place to go. It is encircled by the Elliott Barker State Wildlife Area, the stunningly beautiful Valle Vidal, the magnificent Carson National Forest and the incredible Cimarron Canyon State Park. Biking, hiking, fly-fishing and photography are but a few of the many activities available to you.

Express St. James Hotel

Built between 1870 and 1880 (many say 1872) by French chef Henri (later changed to Henry) Lambert, the Express St. James Hotel continues to be a fine example of enduring workmanship. Lambert, a personal chef of President Abraham Lincoln's, built the St. James on the recommendation of President Ulysses S. Grant. The original name of the hotel was the Lambert Inn; it was changed to the St. James Hotel in later years.

Henry Lambert left his home in Nantes, France, at age twelve to work as an apprentice chef in Le Havre, France. He then joined the French navy and was assigned to that nation's first submarine. A ship towed the submarine to the United States with Henri on board. He joined the Union army and became a cook for Ulysses Grant under the service of President Lincoln. It was after the Civil War that Henri and his wife, Mary, came to New Mexico and settled in Elizabethtown (now a ghost town) to find his fortune in gold. When he found very little gold, Lambert moved to Cimarron at the urging of mega-landowner Lucien B. Maxwell to open the forty-three-room inn. The original hotel was an addition to the saloon and restaurant that the Lamberts already owned.

Mary passed away after the couple had built the St. James Hotel. Henri later met and married his second wife, Mary Elizabeth, in 1883. The couple would raise five sons together in Cimarron.

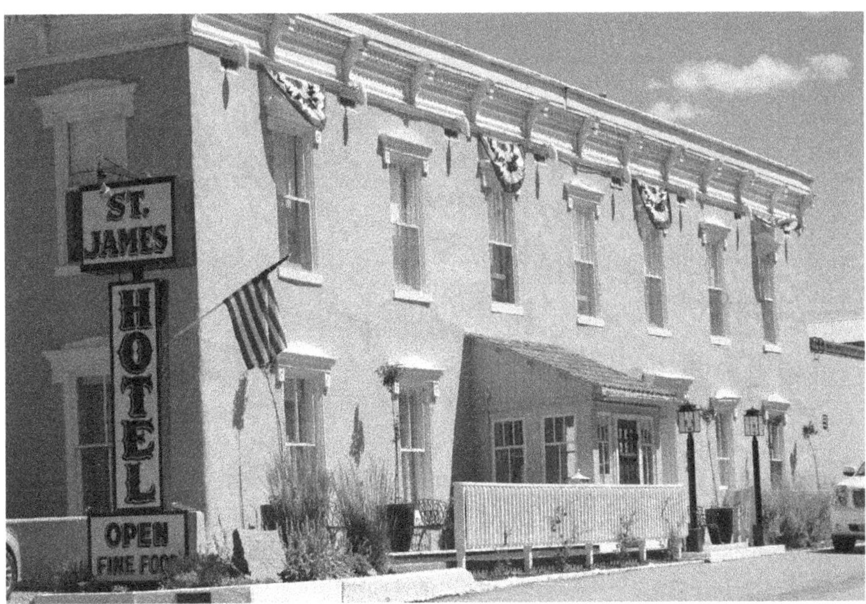

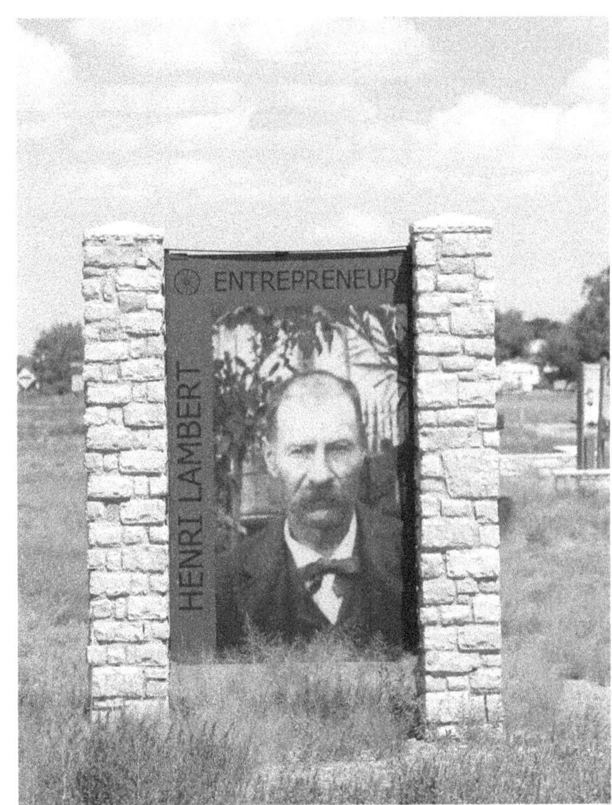

Above: The St. James Hotel has stood on this site since it was built in 1872 and has been used as a central gathering point for many generations. *Courtesy of the author.*

Right: Henri Lambert's portrait stands proudly in the median of U.S. Highway 64 leading into Cimarron. As a founding father of the town, Lambert is highly revered. *Courtesy of the author.*

At least twenty-seven men died in and around the Express St. James Hotel in documented gunfights between 1872 and 1884. Twenty-two visible bullet holes in the bar ceiling are evidence of a much rowdier time in Cimarron, New Mexico, when outlaws roamed the streets itching for a fight. During renovations of the saloon in 1901, the tin ceiling tiles were removed to reveal at least four hundred more bullet holes. It was not uncommon to see at the establishment gunman and local rancher Clay Allison, who allegedly danced on the bar naked while shooting his weapon when he was fully into his drink. It is thought that most of the bullets may have originated from his pistol.

The Express St. James proudly boasts several prominent people from the Old West era who stayed in the hotel and used the ornate wooden staircase to get to their rooms. Among them was William "Buffalo Bill" Cody, who, as a close friend of Henry and Mary Lambert, was present when their son Fred was born in room 31. Cody recruited an entire tribe of Native Americans in Cimarron for his Wild West Show. Another guest was Annie Oakley, who met Cody there several times and planned the Wild West Show as well. Doc Holliday, Bat Masterson and Wyatt Earp also stayed at the hotel. Some think that Jesse James stayed briefly several times, always in room 14, using the alias R.H. Howard. The outlaw "Black Jack" Ketchum is said to have found some peace within the walls of St. James.

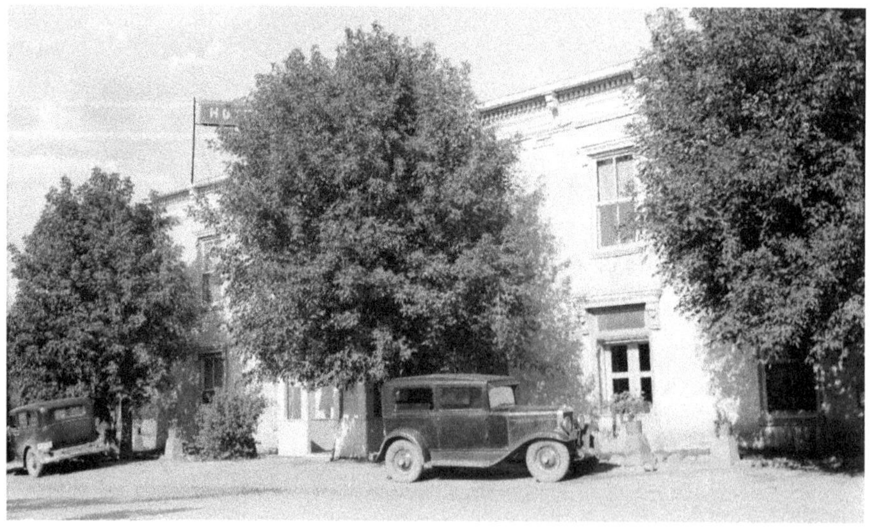

The St. James Hotel had quite a different façade in its earlier years. This would be recognized by the parade of celebrities who stayed there. *Library of Congress.*

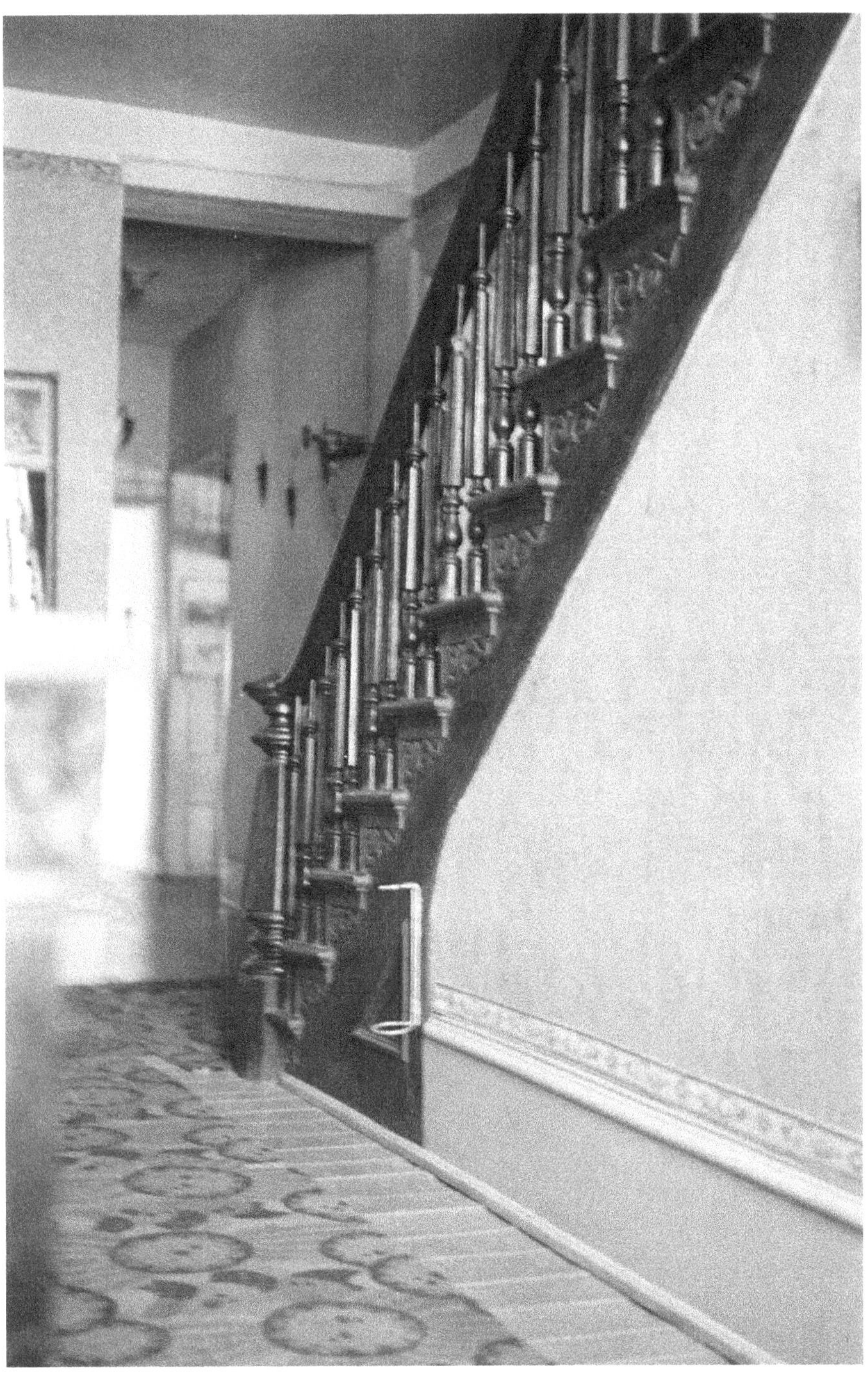

An ornately carved walnut stair railing leads guests to the second floor, where they may or may not encounter an otherworldly experience. *Library of Congress.*

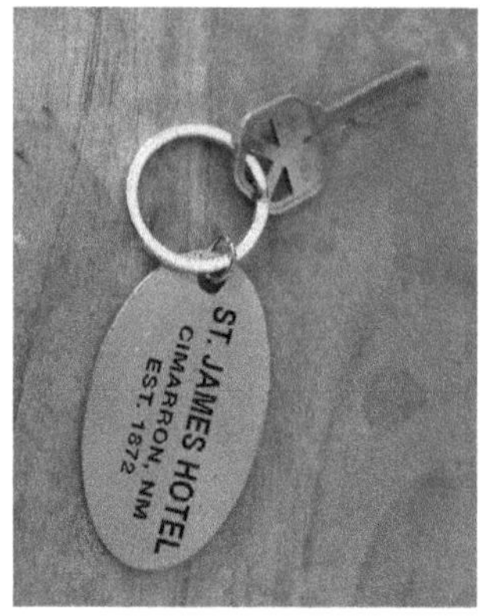

Electronic door locks are not found in the historic St. James Hotel. You will be given a metal key fob emblazoned with the room number. *Courtesy of the author.*

Most of the thirteen historic rooms are named for the famous guests who enjoyed the hospitality of the St. James. Western author Zane Grey was said to have started his novel *Fighting Caravans* in room 22. Author and New Mexico governor Lew Wallace worked on his novel *Ben-Hur* while enjoying the area. Famed artist Frederic Remington spent time in and drew some inspiration from the historic location.

The Express St. James Hotel appears much as it did when first built. The glistening wood floors, plastered walls and wood crown molding harken back to a more elegant, albeit dangerous era. The front lobby is adorned with a mounted bison head, an ornate fireplace with mantle and an original front desk complete with gold security bars. No electronic door locks here, as the rooms are accessed with actual keys with metal key fobs.

As you climb the narrow staircase to the second floor, you will hear a creak or two of protest from the steep wooden stairs. There are no elevators in the original St. James, so if you have trouble climbing stairs, you may want to stay in the modern annex, or, as the staff laughingly calls it, the "sissy wing." That part is not reported to be haunted.

Food service at the Express St. James Hotel has carried on the traditions and talents of its original owner and chef. The menu is full of delicious traditional New Mexican dishes and appetizers, as well as delectable steaks and Angus hamburgers—all with a full bar accompaniment—making the Express St. James the typical hot spot for locals and visitors alike. You can dine inside in one of the historically appointed dining rooms or outside on the beautiful patio accented by a bubbling waterfall and colorful mural. If you play your cards right, on Friday nights, you can enjoy the talents of local musicians as you eat.

One of the most historic rooms of the hotel is the saloon/bar. Do not miss going into this area and counting the many bullet holes in the tin-paneled ceiling. An original roulette wheel that graces the room was widely used by the ruffians who frequented the saloon. The lawlessness prevalent in the region attracted outlaws to the small towns in the New Mexico Territory.

The kind staff members are generous in their willingness to help you. They will make your stay at the Express St. James Hotel a true pleasure.

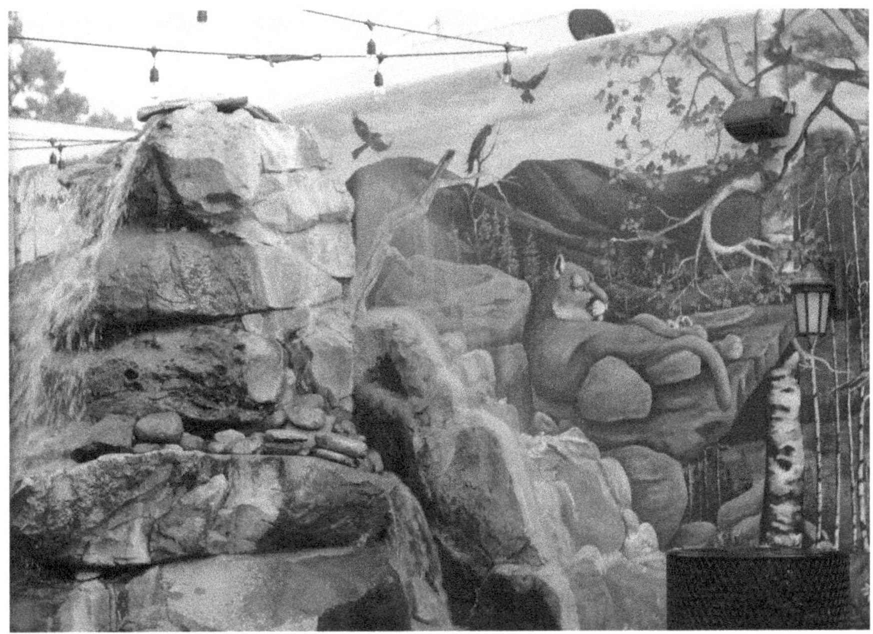

Above: The outdoor patio with fountain is a delightful place to enjoy a meal, a beverage or just listen to the talented musicians. *Courtesy of the author.*

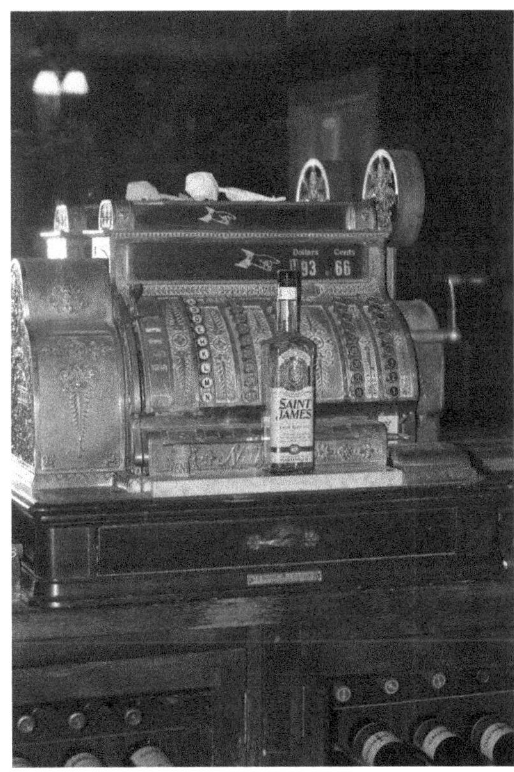

Right: An ornate cash register sits proudly on the hand-carved bar, with a bottle of St. James Whiskey displayed. *Courtesy of the author.*

Ghosts

The Express St. James Hotel is the most documented haunted hotel in New Mexico. As the subject of numerous YouTube videos and Internet discussions, the St. James has garnered great interest from national and international organizations that investigate the paranormal.

The second floor, accessed by a narrow stairway, is known for the most activity. All but one of the rooms are roped off with red velvet barriers, and the doors remain open until occupied. This allows visitors to see and photograph the rooms as they tour the hotel grounds.

Room 18, known as "T.J.'s Room," is the only one that remains closed and padlocked. The public is not allowed within its walls due to the reported powerful nature of the entity that resides there. The staff describes T.J. as an angry, cranky ghost with a history of being violent. Thomas James Wright, a regular at the St. James in the 1880s, would fill his nights playing the house games of faro or poker, smoking cigars and drinking whiskey. Wright's luck significantly turned for the better when he reportedly won ownership of the St. James in a poker game. Happy with his winnings, he returned to his second-floor room to retire for the night. It was there he was shot from behind by an unknown assailant. Barely able to make it the short distance from the doorway to the bed, Wright bled to death there.

The violence and timing of this death would cause anyone to be upset, and he is said to have held a grudge for these many years. Wright's disdain for people in his room is well documented, and the staff is extremely respectful of his feelings by announcing their intentions and asking for permission to enter when they dare. On the extremely rare event that someone is allowed in the room, tokens of appreciation such as small bottles of whiskey, playing cards and cigars are left around the small niche to appease T.J.

Hotel patrons have also taken up the tradition of leaving a shot glass of whiskey on the ledge of the painted transom window as a tribute to the unfortunate cowboy. Sometimes, these full shot glasses are empty by morning, as happened to the author when a full shot glass of whiskey was placed on the transom as a token of thanks for allowing entrance inside his room. The glass was empty the next morning, combined with the strong odor of cigar smoke during the night (being housed in Mary Lambert's room across the hall), even though smoking is not allowed in the hotel. Each made for many theories to fill the mind.

An episode of the television show *Unsolved Mysteries* features the story of the ex-wife of the current owner, who was said to be unhappy about having

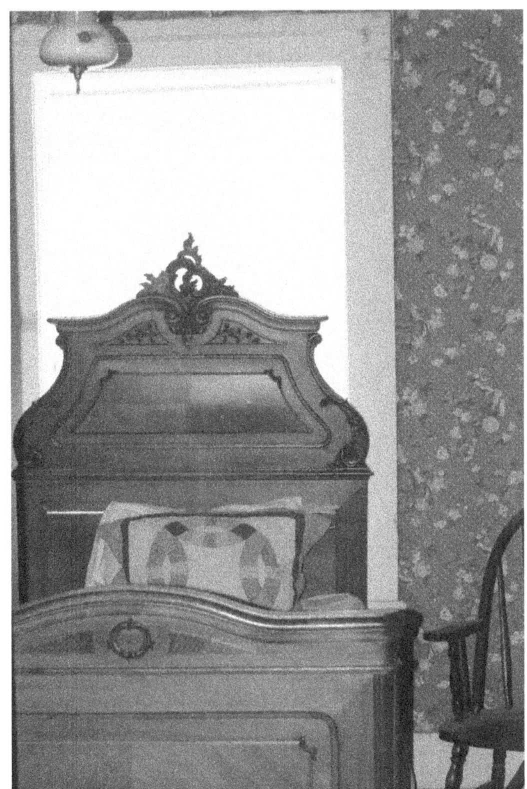

Right: T.J.'s death bed is a narrow wooden bedframe slightly larger than single-occupancy size. Legend says it was here that the gambler took his final breaths. *Courtesy of the author.*

Below: Dust-covered offerings of whiskey, cigarettes and playing cards litter T. J.'s tiny room. They are mementos to appease the angry spirit that resides there. *Courtesy of the author.*

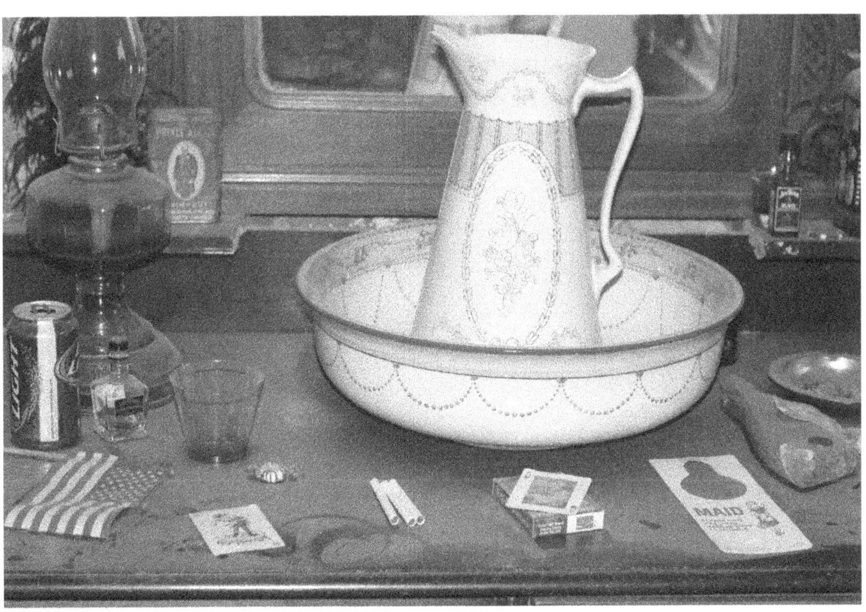

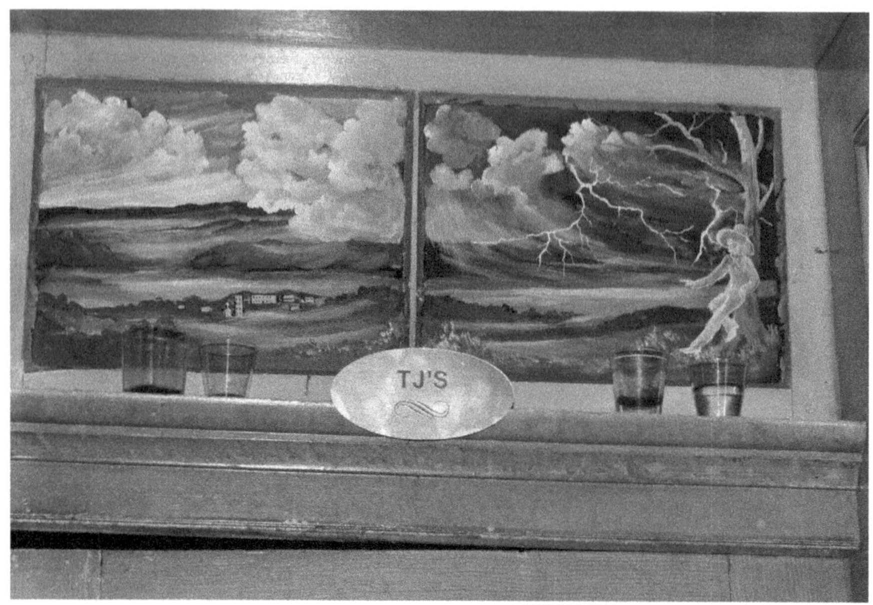

The painted transom window over T.J. Wright's room door is often adorned with shot glasses left by visitors out of respect. *Courtesy of the author.*

the spirits in her hotel. She attempted, from the outside of the St. James Hotel, to tell the paranormal guests that they could leave and to "just go." According to eyewitness accounts, it is said a large orb exited the hotel just long enough to physically knock her down and return into the hotel. Staff members are convinced it was T.J. making his opinion well known.

In Mary Elizabeth Lambert's room 17, across the hall from T.J.'s, occupants often smell a distinctive rose-scented perfume unlike anything manufactured today. It is also reported that Mary likes to play with guests' toes. Guests have claimed to wake up in the middle of the night to the feeling of someone pinching their toes.

There also appears to be a bullet hole in the fine oak floors of Mary's room, although Mary's husband, Henry Lambert, was said to have put extra reinforcements of a double floor to prevent this from happening. Elegant crystal chandeliers grace the upstairs hallway and have been known to turn themselves back on once they were turned off by staff members. They are now kept on, transporting the guest back to an Old West of gunfights, card games and the occasional murder—or two.

The William F. Cody Room, H19, has also had several reports of high activity from otherworldly visitors. Cody was asked by Henri and Mary

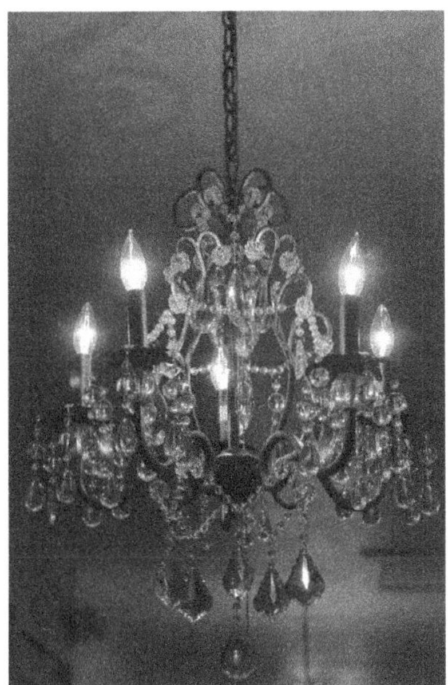

Fine crystal chandeliers illuminate the upstairs hallways, giving a spooky glow to the wood-clad walls. *Courtesy of the author.*

Lambert to be the godfather of their son Fred. Cody later gave lessons to the boy on the use of a weapon.

Giggling children have been heard running up and down the halls when there are none in the hotel at the time. Also, a small, old man—nicknamed the "Little Imp" by the staff—has been seen playing tricks on visitors and staff alike. He also likes to move objects. A handsome face of a cowboy may also appear in an upstairs mirror—be warned.

The Express St. James Hotel has two three-ring binders in the main lobby containing handwritten accounts from patrons of their experiences while staying at the historic hotel. Many of the stories are similar despite being written several years apart. A video is available explaining the various sightings and the degrees to which the owners believe in these happenings.

No matter your belief level, the Express St. James Hotel is certainly the place to go if you want to whet your curiosity for the otherworldly—or to have a full-on encounter. Either way, you will have a wonderful time in these strikingly historic accommodations under the great care of the friendly staff.

7
LAS VEGAS

HISTORIC LAS VEGAS

Las Vegas, New Mexico—not to be confused with its wicked Nevada sister—is situated in a perfect locale for those who want to explore the northern portion of the state. Close to the state capital and to the ski resort town of Taos, as well as to two National Forests, Las Vegas is a blend of college town and historic district. In the 1870s, it was the largest city in the New Mexico Territory.

Founded in 1835 as part of a Mexican Land Grant, Las Vegas began humbly but prospered as a much-needed stop on the Santa Fe Trail. This prosperity came with a price: ruffians. Las Vegas was, in the 1880s, much larger than its counterparts, Santa Fe and Albuquerque, due to the transient nature of the people's existence, making Las Vegas one of the most violent towns in the New Mexico Territory.

Ralph Emerson Twitchell, an early New Mexico historian, described the town: "Without a doubt there is no town which harbored a more disreputable gang of desperadoes and outlaws than did Las Vegas."

As the home of many of President Theodore Roosevelt's Rough Riders, Las Vegas has much to brag about historically. Neighboring Fort Union served as a Civil War post that protected the travelers who made the dangerous trek along the Santa Fe Trail for forty years from 1851 to 1891. The adobe remnants of Fort Union stand today and are available to tour as a national monument. There have been three different versions of the fort

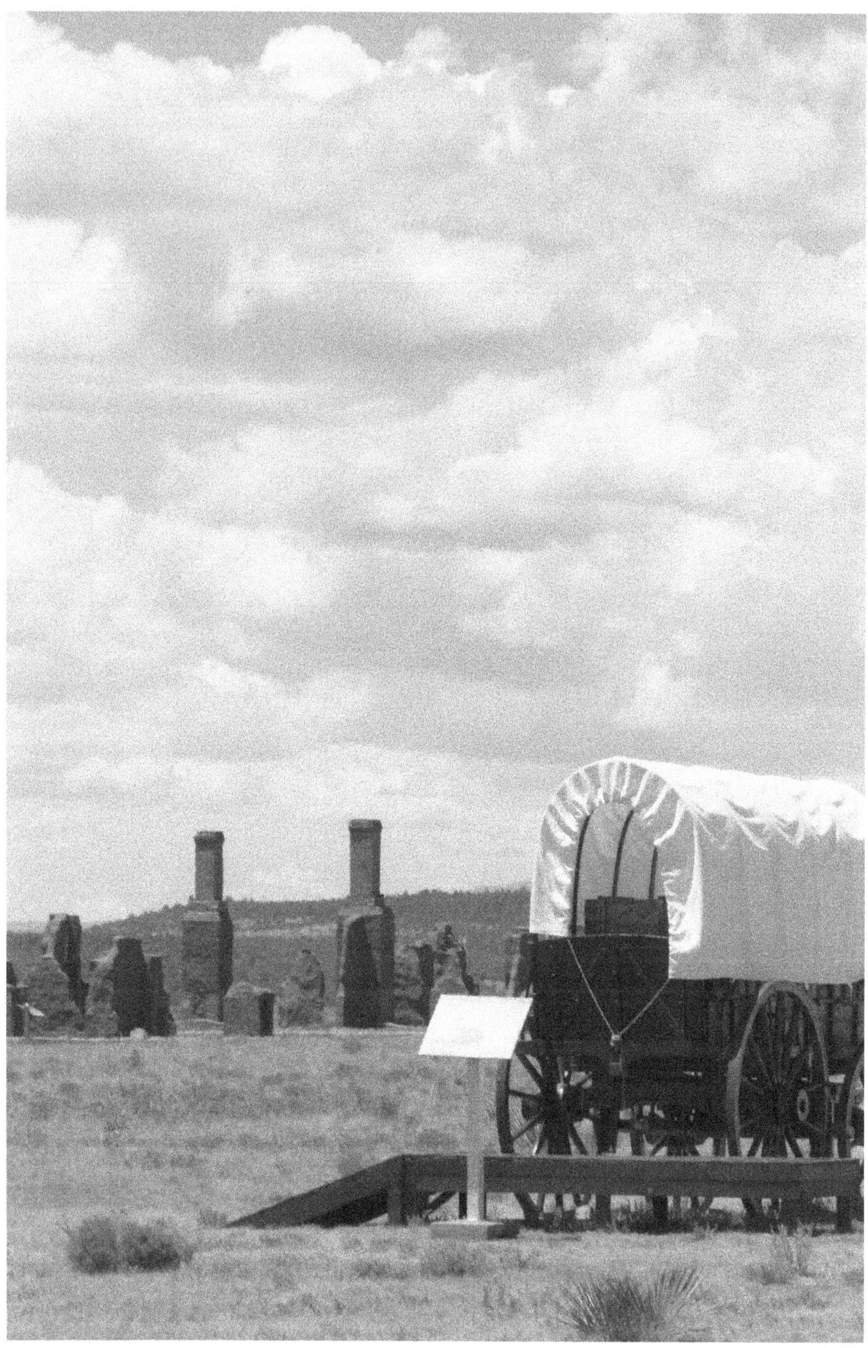

Fort Union, a remote frontier outpost, was built to protect the travelers along the Santa Fe Trail from attacks by indigenous people. *Courtesy of the author.*

on the historic site. The Santa Fe Trail Interpretive Center in Las Vegas gives monthly presentations (March to October) on various subjects involving the fort and the trail.

Las Vegas has played host to a multitude of characters from the Old West, including outlaws Jesse James and Billy the Kid; Confederate spy and shady lady Belle Siddons; lawmen Wyatt Earp, Morgan Earp and Pat Garrett; Theodore Roosevelt; and Indian scout Kit Carson.

In fact, Doc Holliday and his lady, Kate Elder, also known as "Big Nose Kate," set up a saloon and a dental business in downtown Las Vegas before moving on to Dodge City, Kansas, after a gunfight on Centre Street (now Lincoln) in front of his saloon in Las Vegas. The shootout left Army scout Mike Gordon, who was shooting up the establishment, dead, marking Holliday's first killing. The town plaza was the center of commerce and the site of the "hanging tree," which was a windmill frame. It was a constant reminder of the violence that regularly occurred in Las Vegas, as well as a warning to those who might be planning mayhem.

LAS VEGAS TODAY

Home to New Mexico Highlands University, Las Vegas attracts many college students in search of higher education without the difficulty of living in a big city. The campus is nestled in the middle of the Old Town Residential Historic District, which dates to 1840. Las Vegas boasts five historic districts in the confines of its city limits. For anyone interested in architecture, Las Vegas, New Mexico, is a must-see. Represented styles include Queen Anne Victorian, Craftsman, Territorial and Southwestern Adobe.

The La Castañeda Hotel, located by the railroad depot/museum, was once a Harvey House. It is now being renovated to its former Mission-style glory. Las Vegas is also home to a 1904 Carnegie library, located across the street from the Crow's Nest Bed & Breakfast. The Old City Hall has the honor of being the first municipal building erected in New Mexico; it was completed in 1892. To honor Teddy Roosevelt's Rough Riders, Las Vegas has a wonderful museum that tells the history of the First Voluntary Calvary Regiment of the Spanish-American War. Las Vegas was also the site of this group's first reunion.

You will marvel at the number of quaint and unique businesses along Bridge Street near the town plaza. Antiques shops, bookstores, art galleries, nostalgic cafés and an old-fashioned drugstore complete with soda fountains await the visitor who wants to step back into history.

As the location for many movies and television shows, Las Vegas is playing up its appeal to tourists who travel to the town to see the settings of their favorite shows. Signs reading "*Longmire* Fans Welcome" can be found in front of shops encircling the town plaza.

Home to Storrie Lake State Park, Las Vegas provides a beautiful setting to enjoy bird-watching, windsurfing, boating and fishing. It is also a haven for landscape and wildlife photographers.

Also close to Las Vegas are the hot springs—natural thermal pools that visitors can use free of charge. Near the hot springs is the Montezuma Castle, which is now the campus of the Armand Hammer United World College. The castle was built by the Atchison, Topeka & Santa Fe Railway as a luxury hotel. It operated until 1903 and incorporated the hot springs. The Montezuma specialized in treatments for tubercular and other ailments.

When Armand Hammer purchased the property in 1981, he had to do extensive repairs to the historical building, which was placed on the list of America's Most Endangered Historic Places 1997. More than $10 million was spent to bring the building back to life. It has won many historic preservation honors and awards and is designated one of "America's Treasures" by the White House Millennium Council. Today, the building is known as Davis International Center and is not open to the public, but tours are available.

Plaza Hotel 1882

Las Vegas, as the biggest town in the state, needed accommodations, and Benigno Romero took it upon himself to use some of his land-baron cash to build a grand hotel. The Plaza Hotel was completed in 1892 and was called "The Plaza Supper Club," according to the Plaza Hotel website.

Stephen W. Kearney claimed New Mexico for the United States in Las Vegas at the town plaza in 1846, during the Mexican-American War. As the site of President Theodore Roosevelt's Rough Riders reunion in 1899, the Victorian Plaza Hotel has long been the center of the community on the plaza.

The Plaza Hotel looks exactly like it did when it was built. It was often described as the finest hotel in the area and is often referred to as the "Belle of the Southwest." When first erected, it contained a saloon, dance hall

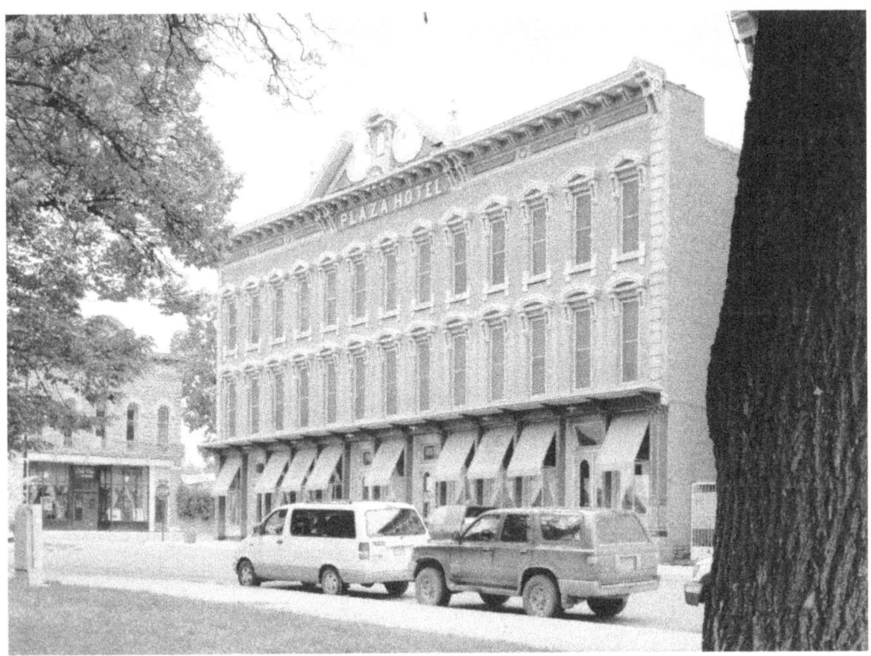

Above: The Plaza Hotel has seen extensive renovations in the interior, but through it all, the exterior remains basically the same as it was when it was built. *Library of Congress.*

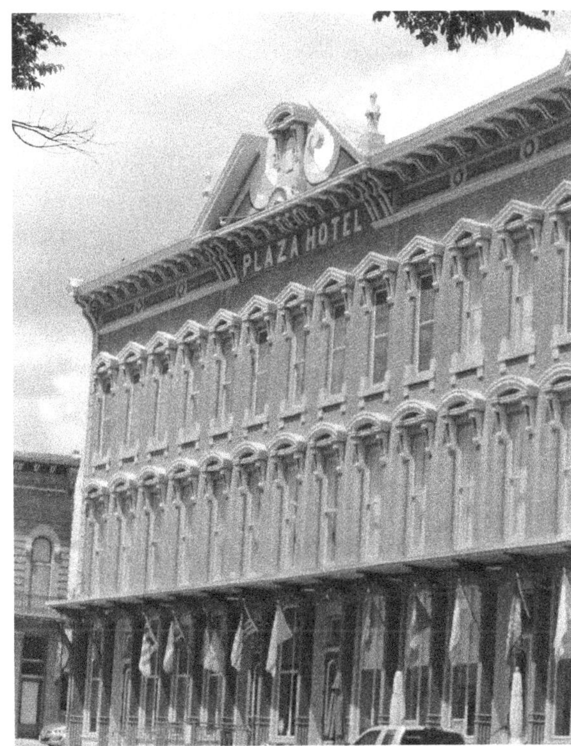

Right: A beautiful façade is the reason the Plaza Hotel is known as the "Belle of the Southwest." Nineteen of the seventy-one rooms overlook the plaza. *Courtesy of the author.*

and restaurant and had thirty-seven guest rooms featuring fourteen-foot ceilings. The Plaza was the place to stay, and it lays claim to have had a host of characters stay under its roof. It is a member of the Historic Hotels of America.

Doc Holliday and Kate Elder moved to Las Vegas and opened a dentist office and a saloon. They were guests of the Plaza Hotel during the planning phase of their adventure. The Plaza Hotel has been the location for many movies and television shows. Dating back to the silent picture days, Tom Mix films were shot here. Moving up to modern times, *Easy Rider*, *Red Dawn*, *Wild Hogs*, *Due Date*, *Beer for My Horses*, *Not Forgotten* and *No Country for Old Men* and the popular television shows *Longmire* and *House of Cards* have all been filmed in and around the Belle, which has seen its share of stars.

In 1982, one hundred years after it was built, the Plaza Hotel received a $1 million face-lift. The Ilfeld Building next door was added to the Plaza Hotel in 2006, adding thirty-five rooms, meeting spaces and a grand ballroom. The Ilfeld Building started its life as the largest department store in the Southwest in 1891.

The Plaza Hotel offers both fine and casual dining for breakfast, lunch and dinner, seven days a week, in an elegantly decorated dining room that looks out on the Las Vegas Plaza. The Plaza Bar offers a peaceful, historical atmosphere to sit and relax to end your day while enjoying your favorite beverage and appetizers. You will find live entertainment every Friday evening starting at 7:30 p.m., and karaoke is available at 7:30 p.m. on Thursday evenings.

Weddings and the Plaza Hotel go hand in hand, not only because of the historic setting but also due to the large banquet room and experienced staff. Grand events here go off without a problem. This opulent room is also the venue for concerts, conventions and banquets on a regular basis.

Be sure to check out the gift shop at the Plaza Hotel during your visit. It offers many unique items for purchase as well as a large variety of books on New Mexico and local history.

GHOSTS

Byron T. Mills was the owner of the Plaza Hotel from approximately 1918 until he died in 1947. The hotel fell into disrepair under his watch; he even thought about razing it in 1940. Thankfully, he decided against that plan, so

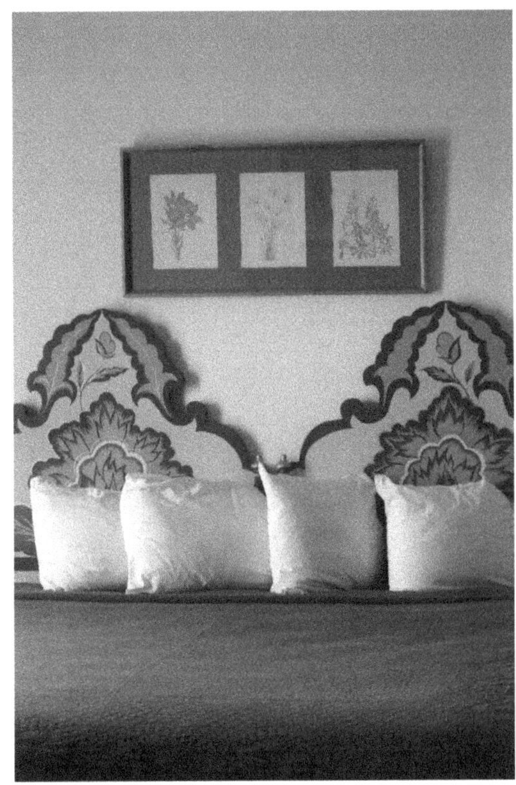

Byron T. Mills's room looks quite different from when the owner stayed there, but he can still be felt prominently on the third floor. *Courtesy of the author.*

we still have the beautiful hotel. Some say that because of his neglect of the hotel and reluctance to fix it the way it deserved, he still wanders the halls out of guilt. Although reported to haunt room 310 generally, as well as 316, his presence has been felt in other rooms as well. Said to prefer the company of single women, mostly redheads, Byron has been known to visit and make his presence known in subtle ways by turning on and off the light or sitting on the bed.

The author had an encounter at the Plaza Hotel with Byron T. Mills in 2007, which led her to further explore the possibility of the existence of otherworldly beings. Traveling by herself, she decided to "test" the stories of the ghost (and, yes, she is a redhead). Asking for a room on the third floor, the author got a sense of being watched the moment the threshold was crossed. Telling herself that she was imagining things, she continued with her evening.

Waking up in the middle of the night, she found she was unable to turn over because of a pressure against the small of her back. Terror instantly rose in her, but she chided herself—this was, after all, what she was wanting.

After a few long moments, she said out loud that she was tired and had a long day ahead of her in the morning and asked to please leave her alone. The pressure was immediately gone, and she did not have the feeling of being watched for the rest of the stay.

Another spirit reported at the Plaza Hotel is that of a small girl who likes the company of women and having her photo taken. She has been captured numerous times sitting next to women in the lobby who are completely unaware of her presence.

Crow's Nest Bed & Breakfast

The Crow's Nest Bed & Breakfast is a striking mixture of several Victorian-era architectural styles and is one of the most notable buildings of its kind in Las Vegas. A three-story Second Empire octagonal tower sets the mood of this Queen Anne house. Built in 1881, the structure was once owned by Dr. H.J. Mueller and his wife, Zella. It is Zella's story we will learn about next.

Mack and Dolly Crow purchased this charming structure in 2000 and have worked hard to maintain the Victorian ambiance by incorporating antiques and original fixtures inside the home. Built by Charles W. Wiley, a railroad grading contractor, the fine building served as his home until 1890, when he sold it to the Muellers. Wiley is said to be credited with bringing the first electric streetlight to Las Vegas and served as the first mayor of East Las Vegas. (Las Vegas is separated east from west by the Gallinas River.)

The Crows say that the Victorian structure has seen many owners as well as many architectural changes. Thankfully, the beautiful home was restored through the efforts of many preservationists in 1996. The Crows owned an insurance and real estate business, which ultimately led them to discover their desire to own a bed-and-breakfast.

Located across the street from Library Park, which is home to one of the few working Carnegie libraries in the country, the Crow's Nest is a good anchor for the corner and keeps watch over the library grounds. The Crow's Nest is a highlight of Victorian architecture and attracts many to Las Vegas, New Mexico, each year just to view the structure.

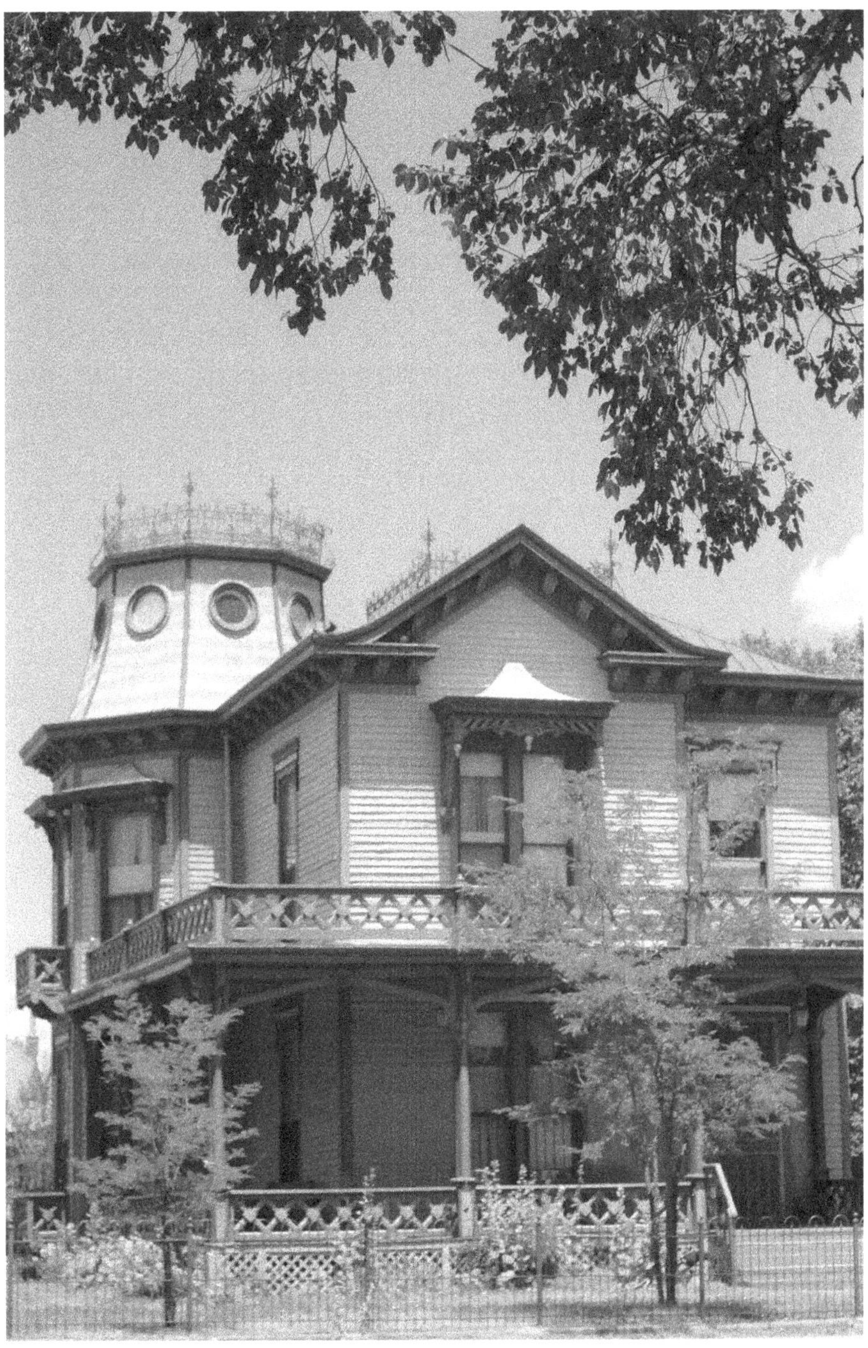

Crow's Nest Bed & Breakfast's exterior is straight out of the Victorian era, complete with gingerbread and widow's walk. *Courtesy of the author.*

GHOSTS

Doctor Henry J. Mueller, the only doctor in Las Vegas, was a jealous man, especially regarding his beautiful wife, Zella. So much so that, it is said, he would not allow her access to the outdoors except to pace the iron-crested widow's walk on the roof of her home. The validity of this story has not been proven. Owner Dolly Crow reported that Zella is a quiet presence and does not make herself known to very many people. A guest from Washington, D.C., did have a brief encounter with Zella when she asked him if he was okay, and she has touched Dolly on the shoulder.

Another spirit thought to be in the Crow's Nest is Zella's son, who, it was said, also died in the house at an early age. He is a more playful spirit and loves children. The owner's young nephew came to visit one summer and became frustrated whenever he saw the little boy and no one else could. The spirit so enjoyed his time playing that he followed the family to their home out of state and caused a bit of havoc there, until he was told to go home—which he did.

When Mack and Dolly's grandchildren were young (under ten), the ghostly activity was at an elevated level. One story goes that every time their granddaughter would say "Boo!" the smoke alarm would go off and cartoons would be playing on every television channel when the children were in the room.

Dolly reported that, last summer, she decided to do some furniture rearranging in the master bedroom. After she completed the task of moving a chair away from a certain wall, she saw two men in military uniforms walk through the room later that night. One took two steps into the room, looked at the bed and walked away. The other walked in and continued without acknowledging the surroundings. Dolly feels she may have opened a temporary portal for the gentlemen to use; she had heard that the grounds on which the Crow's Nest was built may have contained a cemetery at one time, moved many years ago for development.

All in all, the spirits that reside in the Crow's Nest are very gentle and are approved by the family dog, who is always wagging his tail vigorously while staring into space.

8
LINCOLN

HISTORIC LINCOLN

Lincoln, New Mexico, a one-street town, was given the dubious honor of being called the "most dangerous street in America" by President Rutherford Hays. Gunfights were common occurrences along this stretch of road and a favorite stomping ground for Lincoln County's favorite outlaw, William H. McCarty/Antrim/Bonney, a.k.a., "the Kid"—later known as "Billy the Kid."

As residents like to say, "many murders and much mayhem" occurred along this short stretch of road in the middle of the picturesque Capitan Mountains. Land struggles, cattle rustling, hatred and prejudice fueled some of the deadliest battles fought at the time. The famous Lincoln County War was fought over cattle contracts with the government in neighboring Fort Stanton.

The outlaw William H. Bonney, a.k.a. Billy the Kid, was a force to be reckoned with in these parts, and he was quite celebrated even in his own time. Although little is known about the Kid's early life, it is widely stated that he was born William Henry McCarty Jr. in New York City on November 23, 1859. For unknown reasons, William's mother, Catherine, moved William and his older brother, Joseph, west, stopping in several midwestern states along the way to seek work. Eventually, the family stopped in Santa Fe, New Mexico, where Catherine met and married Billy's stepfather, William Antrim.

Billy's life would turn tragic at the tender age of fourteen, when his mother succumbed to tuberculosis while living in Silver City, New Mexico, in 1874, leaving Billy and Joseph to fend for themselves as teenagers; their stepfather was not interested in raising the two boys. Billy is thought to have committed his first murder in Silver City before escaping to Arizona. After maturing a bit, Billy returned to New Mexico and settled into the south-central/southeastern section of the state, where he worked as a cowboy for the largest cattle owner in the state, John Simpson Chisum.

The five-day battle known as the Lincoln County War was fought by two factions who were vying for the right to supply nearby Fort Stanton with meat and other sundries. Since Jimmy Dolan and Lawrence Murphy were immigrants from Ireland, a holdover of the tensions there may have contributed to the hatred they felt for the newcomer, John Tunstall, who happened to be English. The Murphy & Dolan Mercantile and Bank, or "the House," was the only store in Lincoln County, the largest county in the New Mexico Territory at that time. The Murphy-Dolan faction was in complete control of pricing and supply; as a result, they were able to take in huge profits. Tunstall's store, the H.H. Tunstall & Company Store, was a threat to their comfortable livelihood.

The Englishman was befriended by a young Gaelic- and Spanish-speaking man—later known as "Billy the Kid"—who worked cattle for him in the Hondo Valley. Billy grew fond of his employer, who had treated him kindly, and Billy would come to think of the Englishman as a father figure. These ill feelings escalated and came to an apex with the murder of John Tunstall on February 18, 1878. This killing, widely thought to have been conducted by members of the Murphy-Dolan group, sparked the formation of the "Regulators," which included Billy the Kid as their leader. The Regulators sought to avenge the death of their boss and brought the battle to the streets of Lincoln.

The battle raged for five days and resulted in the deaths of five Regulators, including attorney Alexander McSween. His house, where the Regulators were hold up, was burned to the ground. The Murphy-Dolan faction suffered only one death and several men wounded. In total, nineteen people lost their lives in the intense fighting. With the arrival of the U.S. Calvary from Fort Stanton to put an end to the fighting, Billy the Kid left Lincoln with revenge on his mind.

Territorial Governor Lew Wallace (author of *Ben-Hur*) wanted to impose martial law on Lincoln to stop the war, but President Hayes advised against it, suggesting that those involved be given amnesty. Wallace complied, and amnesty was given—to all except Billy the Kid. Billy would write numerous letters after the Lincoln County War to Governor Wallace to gain amnesty but never lived to see it happen.

Waging a personal war on those he thought responsible for his friend's death, Billy formed the Billy the Kid Gang, often referred to as the "Rustlers." They plagued cattle baron John S. Chisum to the point that he had an active hand in the election of Pat Garrett as sheriff of Lincoln County, who was immediately given the task of bringing his once friend to justice. Garrett would accomplish this task in Fort Sumner, New Mexico, on July 14, 1881, in the home of Pete Maxwell, brother of Lucien Maxwell of Maxwell Land Grant fame.

Pat Garrett's actions were called heroic by those suffering the effects of Billy's cattle rustling, but the townspeople, especially the Hispanic population, had a great hatred for Garrett after that. The six-foot, five-inch Pat Garrett was known as an unlucky lawman. He was eventually killed on his way by buckboard to Las Cruces, New Mexico, in 1908 by Wayne Brazeal, a Billy the Kid sympathizer.

Lincoln Today

As you turn to the right off Highway 70, which continues toward Ruidoso, and meander along the narrow road that is Highway 380, you will swear that you crossed a time warp. Lincoln, New Mexico, has been described as "history frozen in time." The two-lane road that winds through the peaceful valley will lure you in with scenic views of the Capitan Mountains and Smokey the Bear country.

Be prepared to be amazed when you notice the historical Territorial style and adobe structures that make up the town. The quaint cemetery on the edge of town has graves dating back to the 1880s with headstones carved by Robert "Bob" Brookshire, a stonemason and later hermit of McKittrick Cave near Carlsbad. A sign depicting a horse and buggy will greet you, and do not be surprised if you see such a rig parked on the side of the road.

The buildings that line the sleepy street of Lincoln, New Mexico, look much as they would have in 1870, at the height of the hamlet's existence—especially the Torreon, which is a round adobe structure in the middle of town. The cross cutouts located in all directions on the Torreon were for

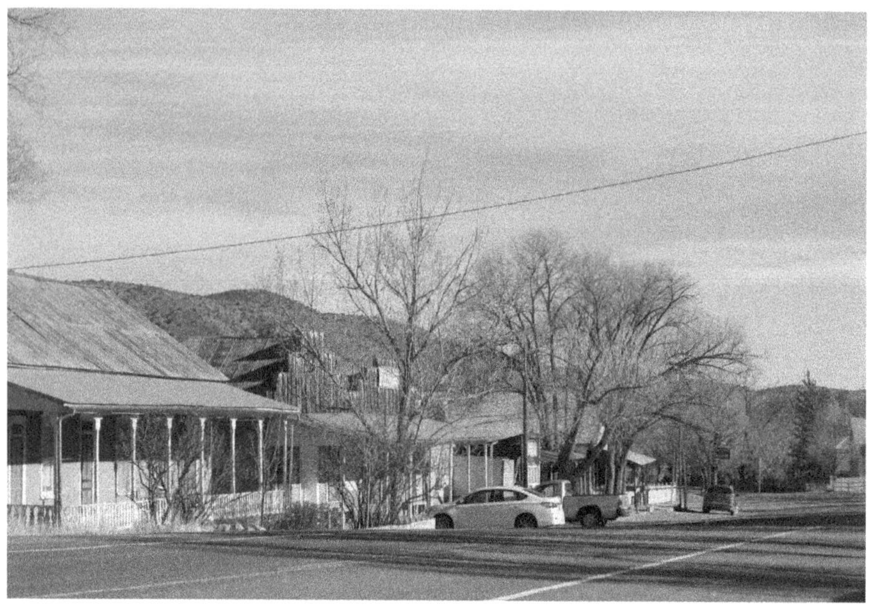

Modern-day Lincoln, New Mexico, looks extremely similar to how it would have appeared when Billy the Kid sauntered up the road. *Courtesy of the author.*

the men to position their rifles in defense of Lincoln during attacks by the Mescalero Apache tribe, which lived in the nearby mountains.

If Billy the Kid were to walk down the main street of Lincoln, New Mexico (the town was originally called La Placitas del Rio Bonito), he would be surprised at how many of his old haunts he would be able to completely recognize. Many of the forty-eight historic buildings have been lovingly restored to their original luster after age, natural destruction and the Lincoln County War had taken their tolls. Many quaint businesses have utilized these buildings for coffee shops and gift shops. Recently, Lincoln has seen a resurgence in interest from the public and is catering to this by providing "Lincoln After Dark" tours throughout the year. These events are sponsored by the Friends of Lincoln County and the Lincoln County Museum.

Lincoln is a state monument. It was declared a National Historic Landmark in 1960 and is in the National Register of Historic Places. It is regulated by the State of New Mexico, and for a small entry fee, you can tour the historic buildings to get a profound sense of the past and of the characters who formed the saga. Each structure has a rich story to tell, and the Lincoln County Museum is a must-see and a good place to start and finish your

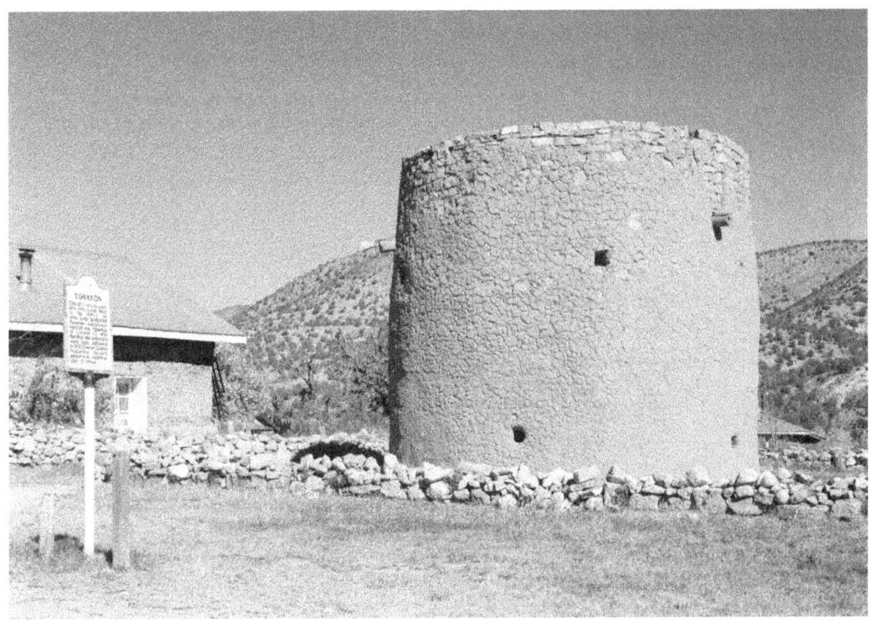

This round, twenty-foot adobe structure in the center of town was used for defense against the Mescalero Apaches. The entire town would huddle in the Torreon for refuge. *Library of Congress.*

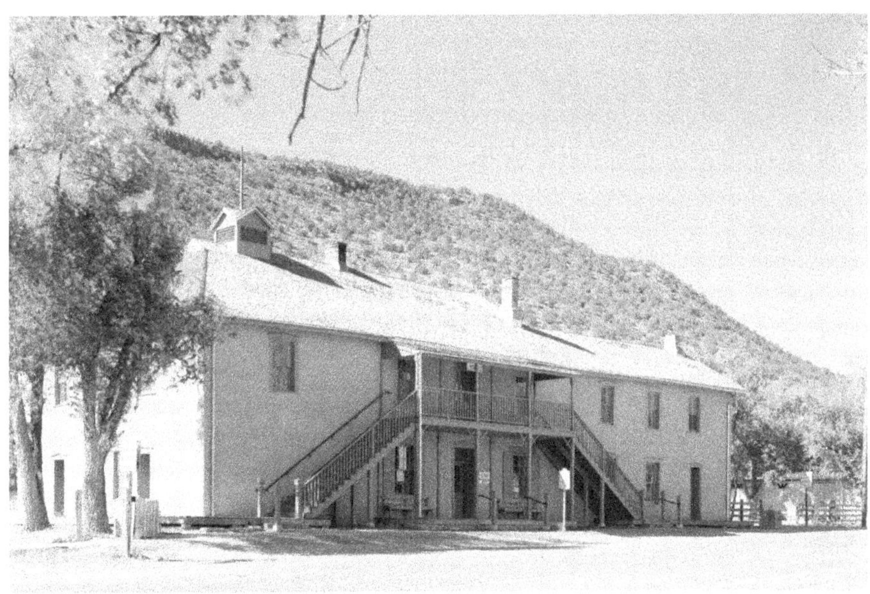

The Lincoln County Courthouse once housed Billy the Kid on murder charges and was the site of one of his most daring escapes, in 1881. *Library of Congress.*

journey through times gone by. Character actors wander the streets giving tidbits of history to and taking photos with those who pass by.

Luckily, Lincoln is operated by the Lincoln Historic Site, which includes a fascinating museum that brings the events of Lincoln to life. Docents and guides will give you a tour of the historic site during special events; otherwise, you are able to walk the "most dangerous street" at your leisure and soak in the ambiance of one of the last remaining examples of the Old West in a noncommercial condition.

Be sure to look for the two wooden crosses located behind Tunstall's Store in Lincoln. They were placed there as a commemoration of the deaths of two of the most well-known victims of the Lincoln County War: John Tunstall and attorney Alexander McSween. Although the two are not buried under these crosses, it is said that they are buried in a secret cemetery on the Amistae family property next door. Be sure to ask about them, but please do not wander into the backyard directly next door.

Lincoln comes to life in the spring as reenactments of famous gunfights occur on the narrow street. Every first weekend of August, "Billy the Kid" comes to visit and to participate in "The Last Escape of Billy the Kid" as part of Old Lincoln Days and the Billy the Kid Pageant, which draws hundreds of visitors to the sleepy village with parades, food vendors and people in period clothing to marvel at the hijinks of New Mexico's favorite boy bandit.

The Dolan House

The home of Lincoln County War participant James "Jimmy" Dolan, this quaint adobe home served James and his family well since its construction in 1883. Today, there is only one room to rent, but the atmosphere and ambiance of the room recalls the 1880s. A large four-poster bed appointed in rich burgundy linens is the focal point, flanked by an original fireplace and a private screened-in porch.

Jimmy Dolan, born in Galway, Ireland, was known to have a bad temper and was thought to have been involved in several killings and attempted murders during his years in Lincoln. An attempt on a Fort Stanton captain, James Randlett, landed Dolan and his business partner, Lawrence "L.G." Murphy, owner of L.G. Murphy & Co. Store, in enough hot water that Murphy was banned from Fort Stanton due to Dolan's actions.

Both Dolan and Murphy served in the Union army and had served at Fort Stanton, where they met. Murphy had a sutler store that supplied Fort Stanton and the local native tribe, the Mescalero Apaches. Because it was the only store in the area, the owner was awarded these lucrative contracts. Trouble brewed for the Irishman when it was discovered that much of the beef he supplied was illegally obtained. Fort officials accused the store of price gouging and scamming the Mescaleros. Somehow, Murphy kept his contracts and planned to expand his business in Lincoln.

After opening the "Murphy & Dolan Mercantile and Banking" building in Lincoln, the pair was able to obtain a government contract with Fort Sumner—but they continued to conduct bad business practices. Poor farmers were forced to do business with the store and pay the prohibitive costs, which angered them, making the owners widely detested in the community. These tensions were the foundation for the developing Lincoln County War strife. The two men were known to have connections with the "Santa Fe Ring."

When the competing store owner, John Tunstall, was killed—widely thought under the orders of Murphy and Dolan—adding insult to murder, Dolan purchased Tunstall's ranch and store. Dolan went on to serve as the treasurer for Lincoln County and to serve in the Territorial Senate. He passed away on February 6, 1898, at age forty-nine on his ranch after acquiring all of Tunstall's property. His death was widely rumored to be caused by heavy alcoholism, which had consumed him all his life.

Dolan House was built between 1883 and 1884 by a French Canadian from Vermont, George Peppin (soon to be sheriff) and carpenter Elijah Dow. This same duo is responsible for building San Juan Catholic Church, Dr. Wood's house and the famous courthouse in Lincoln.

According to the current owners, Beverly and Bill Strauser, Jimmy Dolan had more than twenty thousand adobe bricks specially made to construct his beautiful home. The original structure consisted of six rooms with an entryway. As with the custom of the day, the walls were more than twenty inches thick, forming an excellent barrier against the elements. Adobe structures are celebrated for being warm in the winter and cool in the summer, a result of this architectural feature. Each of the fourteen-by-fourteen-foot rooms featured a twelve-foot ceiling as well.

A breezeway was constructed between the main house and the summer kitchen and served the Dolan family as an outdoor dining area. A hand-dug, fifty-foot well was rock-lined to the bottom and supplied the home with much-needed water. The recent addition of a pump to the well is used to water the surrounding grounds.

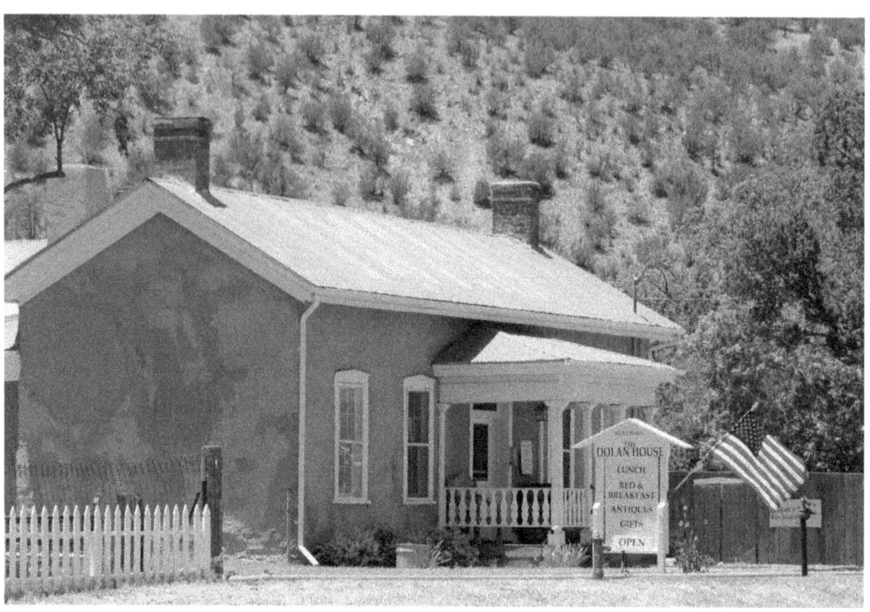

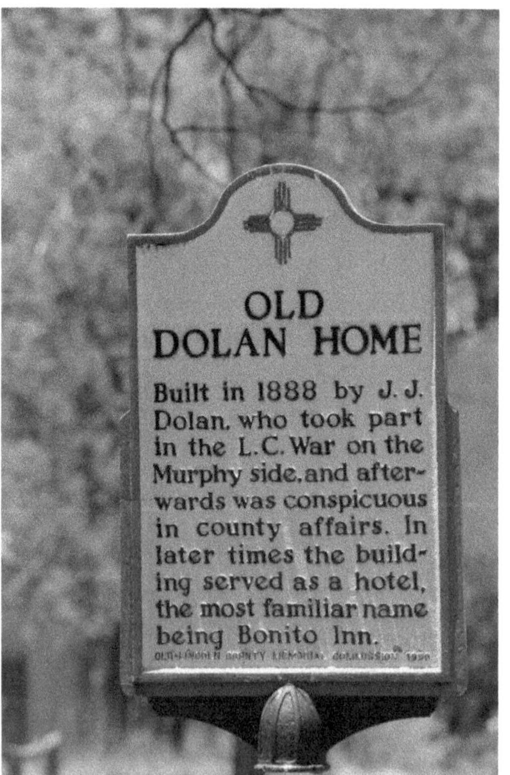

Above: The Dolan House is made from twenty thousand adobe bricks, forming one of the finest homes in Lincoln. *Courtesy of the author.*

Left: The historical marker of the Dolan House tells of its fascinating history and that of the Lincoln County War. *Courtesy of the author.*

When the Dolan House became the Bonito Inn in the 1920s, the large breezeway porch was closed in and now serves as the dining room. While researching his role in the movie *Billy the Kid*, Douglas Fairbanks stayed at the Dolan House to soak in the history. During this time, the Dolan House had a picket fence, which Fairbanks used to scale instead of using the gate, much to the amusement of the locals.

Since 1950, the Dolan House has grown to a total of thirteen rooms and a square footage of more than four thousand. Beverly and Bill Strauser bought Dolan House in 2007 and have lovingly restored the structure to look much as it did when Jimmy Dolan strolled through the rooms. The Strausers provide delicious meals and homemade ice cream—and some of the best pie in the county.

A historical marker tells the story of the Dolan House for the many visitors who stroll past the home each day. The peaceful setting is a far cry from the violence this humble abode witnessed in its past.

Ghosts

Tragedy befell the Dolan family on several occasions, according to an unpublished manuscript by author Charles L. Usmar III, who has done extensive research on the family.

Jimmy Dolan, thirty-one, married eighteen-year-old Caroline Fritz in 1879—even for those times, it was a significant difference in age. Caroline's Lutheran family was not happy with her marrying into the Catholic faith and did not attend the wedding. Although there was religious tension, Caroline's father, Charles Fritz, allowed the newly married couple to live at his ranch (Spring Ranch) near Lincoln until their home was completed in 1883. A son and a daughter were born to the couple while at Spring Ranch. Two other children, two daughters, would be born in their new home.

Born in 1880, Emil Dolan passed away at the age of two from disease and was buried in the Fritz Cemetery on Spring Ranch. Dolan's second daughter, Louise Mabel, also died from disease at the newly constructed home in 1883, to be followed by their mother in 1886 after the birth of the last daughter, Bessie. All of the Dolans were buried in the Fritz Cemetery.

During Caroline's last extremely difficult pregnancy, Jimmy decided to bring in a nanny and housekeeper from Fort Stanton to help. Maria Whitlock stayed with Caroline until her death in 1886 from childbirth and continued living in the house for a year and a half to help raise Bessie. Jimmy and Maria were married at the Dolan House in Lincoln by Elijah Long, chief justice of the New Mexico Territorial Supreme Court, in 1888.

The presence of Caroline is felt in the room that once served as her bedroom, which is also the room rented out by the Strausers. One can image how Caroline must have felt with another woman sharing the home she had built with her husband. This may be the reason she still resides there.

The Wortley Hotel: A Historic Bed-and-Breakfast

Come and relax on the ninety-two-foot-long front porch of the famous hotel that has seen many a shoot-out and played host to lawmen and ruffians since its opening in 1874. It was once owned by famed lawman Pat Garrett, who reportedly purchased the property for $275. He would go on to claim the life of outlaw Billy the Kid. Although the Wortley Hotel has seen many name changes and owners and burned down a couple of times, its proprietors always provided hot meals and clean accommodations for weary travelers then and history enthusiasts today.

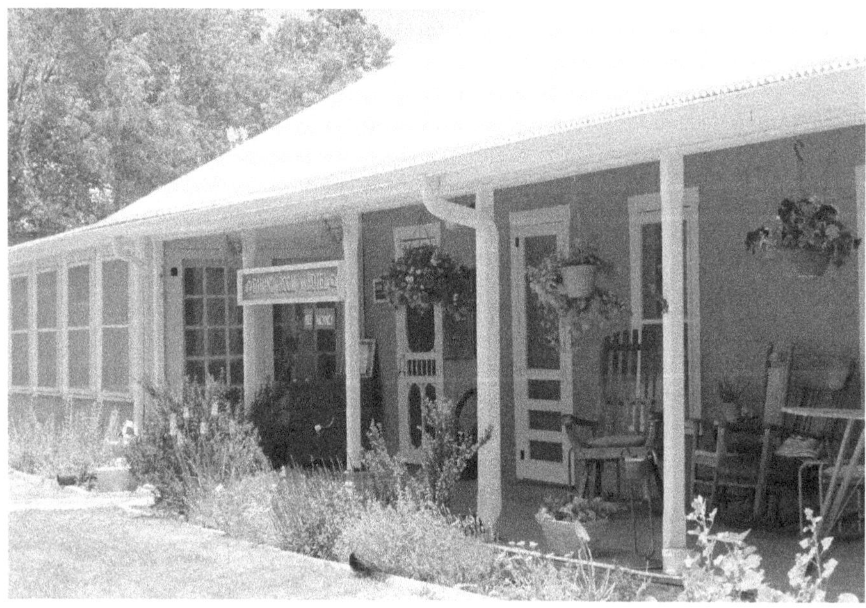

The Wortley Hotel exterior porch is more than ninety-two feet long and furnished with heavy rocking chairs for the comfort of its guests. *Courtesy of the author.*

Today's accommodations include a working fireplace in each of the five rooms, which also have private entrances and bathrooms. Four of the historical rooms feature queen-sized beds; the other has a full-sized mattress with a twin-sized roll-away bed. There are no televisions in the rooms, which the owners believe adds to the setting's tranquility. The Wortley Hotel is proud to be a green establishment and uses only home-manufactured soaps and cleaning supplies. Each room has the Wortley-made goat's-milk soap, emblazoned with the signature "W."

The hotel supports quite a menagerie of farm animals. The free-range chickens—called the Wortley Welcoming Committee—will most likely greet you as you walk up to the property. Be nice to them, for they will be providing your breakfast. A mini-farm behind the Wortley houses goats, pigs and sheep. Natural wildlife will most certainly visit, so be prepared to see some of the resident deer and elk on the front lawn.

While rocking in the heavy wooden rocking chairs on the front porch, close your eyes and take in the cool mountain air. You will almost hear a time a century ago when New Mexico was just a territory and was a perfect place for those seeking to hide out in the beautiful Capitan Mountains. It's hard to imagine that this tranquil setting was the location of so much violence, when tempers were quick and pistols even quicker.

Originally built in 1872, the Wortley Hotel, named after the hotel's former owner and cook, Sam Wortley, housed the workers who were erecting a two-story building across the street: "Murphy's Big Store," owned by another Lincoln County War participant, Lawrence Murphy. He was partners with Jimmy Dolan. The Big Store later became the Lincoln County Courthouse, the site of one of Billy the Kid's most daring escapes.

Deputy Sheriff Ameredith Robert "Bob" Olinger was seated for lunch at the Wortley Hotel on April 28, 1881, when he was alerted by shots fired at the courthouse. Billy had just shot Deputy James Bell after tricking the lawman with a trip to the outhouse, where he allegedly obtained a weapon. Billy then waited on the second floor of the courthouse for his nemesis, Bob Olinger, to appear in the street. Olinger was known to have taunted the Kid during his incarceration at the Lincoln County Courthouse, causing a huge amount of resentment to pile up in the young outlaw. Olinger, sometimes described as a "bully with a badge" in texts, is not highly regarded by history.

As Olinger crossed the street from the Wortley Hotel, he heard Billy say, according to witnesses, "hello, Bob." When the lawman looked up, he was shot with his own double-barrel shotgun. Olinger went down in history as the last man to die at Billy's hand. The Wortley Hotel had a special in the restaurant of pot roast and mashed potatoes in honor of the last meal Olinger was not able to finish, even though it is not quite certain what he ordered. In April 1878, Sheriff William Brady enjoyed a great breakfast at the Wortley Hotel shortly before he was shot eleven times by the Regulators as he did his morning rounds of Lincoln. The owners are also quick to add that "no guests have been gunned down in 135 years."

The Wortley Hotel was also the headquarters for Sheriff George Peppin and his deputies during the Lincoln County War. They also had half a dozen men stationed in the nearby Torreon. The hotel also hosted many of the famous players of the New Mexico Territory, such as judges, lawyers and law enforcement officers, as they traveled to Lincoln for court hearings.

Today's owners, Troy Nelson and Katherine Marsh, are proud to be able to offer guests a comfortable, historical bed-and-breakfast hotel where they can enjoy the beautiful countryside of Lincoln and all the modern amenities they expect.

> *Today, as a Bed and Breakfast hotel, we treat you with the finest 21st century standards while maintaining the Wortley's historic character. If you're searching for the fading antiquity and authenticity of America's West coupled with a comfortable stay in antique filled lodgings and capped off with excellent meals, we invite you to give us a call or send an email. You'll enjoy your stay with us and we'll look forward to your next visit. Lincoln will take you back in time and the Wortley will admirably add the finishing touches!*

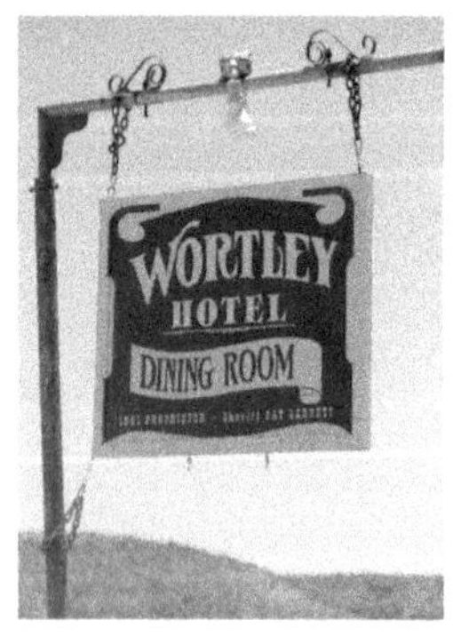

The Wortley Hotel sign welcomes its guests much as it did when it was owned by Sheriff Pat Garrett. *Courtesy of the author.*

The Worley Hotel states on its website that gila monsters (poisonous lizard), rattlesnakes, buffalo and bears were once menu options; rest assured, these are no longer offered on the menu. A freshly cooked breakfast of eggs, bacon, pancakes, home fries and berries is included in the room rate. The Wortley Hotel will also work closely with you if you have a food allergy or special diet. The hotel prefers to use locally grown culinary items for its menu. You can choose from a widely varied menu and dine on barbeque pork sandwiches, a Caprese salad and chocolate mousse, all within a few steps from where so much history was made.

The lazy Rio Bonito winds behind the Wortley Hotel and down through the Hondo Valley, where it merges with the Rio Ruidoso. At one time, the Rio Bonito—more a creek than a river that begins on the mighty Sierra Blanca—was a hotbed of activity. Gold was discovered in its silt, precipitating a gold rush in the area. Today, the setting is a perfect place to rest your soul and rejuvenate your weary spirit.

GHOSTS

Many guests have walked into the doors of the Wortley Hotel straight out of history, and it is thought that some of them enjoyed staying so much that they do not want to leave.

The owners have reported hearing disembodied voices and having items disappear, only to reappear in a different spot. Cold spots are widely reported throughout the hotel that cannot be linked to the age of the Wortley.

Guests have reported seeing apparitions of men in long black coats floating along the hallway or inside their rooms. Many believe these could be the spirits of Deputy Bell and Olinger, who were shot just outside the hotel in the 1880s by Billy the Kid. Or perhaps it is Sheriff William Brady, who also met his fate on the street in front of the Wortley Hotel, supposedly by Billy's hand.

Since the Wortley Hotel was used as a military headquarters during the five-day battle of the Lincoln County War, soldiers have been seen crossing the grounds. A ghostly herd of horses can sometimes be heard as they travel up the Rio Bonito toward Fort Stanton.

9

CHAMA

Historic Chama

The Chama Valley has a long and proud history dating back to ancient man more than one thousand years ago. The indigenous peoples of the region established the Puye Cliff Dwellings (in the Tewa language, "pueblo ruin where the rabbits assemble or meet"). Today, the Cliff Dwellings are a national landmark and are operated and owned by the Santa Clara Pueblo. The Tewa people built the one-story adobe pueblos close to the cliff dwellings, which were carved out of the Puye Mesa by the Anasazi. The cliff dwellings were once inhabited by an estimated 1,440 people, who lived there from the 1100s until it was abandoned in 1580. Later, the Jicarilla Apaches became the most influential indigenous group to inhabit the Chama Valley after they migrated from Colorado. Evidence of their cultural influences are still present.

Chama was first settled as a Hispanic town named San Joaquin del Rio de Chama. According to the records of the New Mexico state historian Francisco Salazar, his two brothers and another group of citizens filed a petition with Territorial Governor Joaquin Real Alancaster to give them a vacant section of land along the Rio Chama. The petition, known as the Cañon de Chama Grant, was approved on August 1, 1806, and an agricultural settlement began, only to be abandoned for a short time due to attacks from local tribes. But by 1861, the original thirty-one land grant recipients had grown to more than four hundred.

Railroad workers soon came to the area in droves and set up a large tent city, allowing them to work on the expanding railroad system. The post office soon opened under the name "Chama" in 1880. Miners came to the town on their way to Silverton and Leadville, Colorado, to work in the many mines there.

The headwaters of the mighty Rio Chama converged with the Rio Grande to carve out the lush valley and formed two of New Mexico's largest lakes, the Heron and El Vado, which are now New Mexico state parks. Water from these sources was used for irrigation by the native people and those who followed to grow their crops to sustain them through the frigid winters.

During the construction of the Denver and Rio Grande Railroad in the 1880s, Chama, located in Rio Arriba County, grew by leaps and bounds, attracting new residents who wanted to grasp the opportunities the town had to offer. Most of these people were beneficial to the town, while others were a bit on the shady side. The lumbermen, engineers and laborers needed a place to stay and carouse, so Foster's Hotel was a perfect site.

Clay Allison, a notorious gunman who terrorized much of the state of New Mexico, was known to enjoy the less "civilized" parts of the territory,

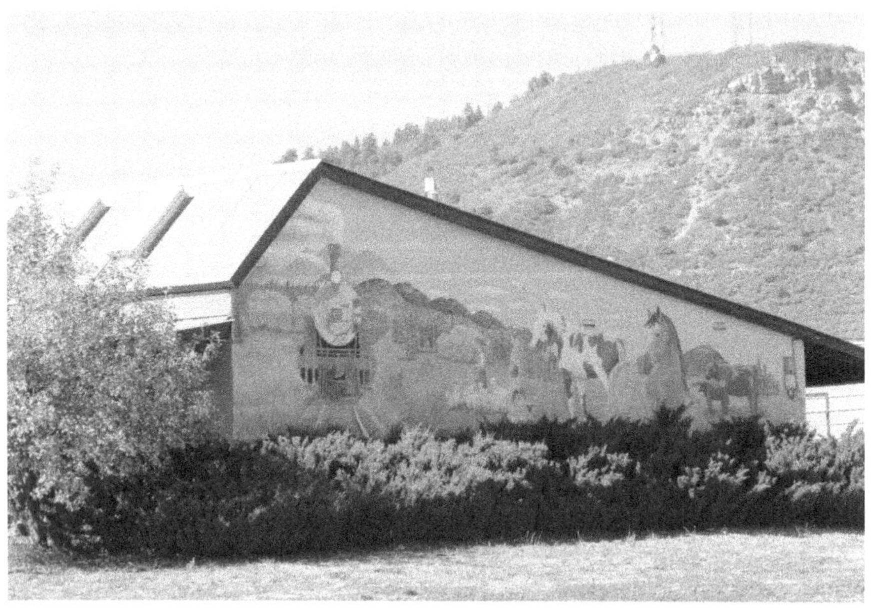

A mural of all that is important to the village of Chama shows farming, ranching, native cultures and the railroad. *Courtesy of the author.*

where the law was scarce. Chama fit the bill. As a raucous young town, Chama had a reputation as a place with many saloons, a gambling house and even moonshine stills. This attracted the outlaw, who was said to have held up railroad pay cars and construction camp payrolls on a regular basis. But when the boom left Chama, so did most of the town's more colorful citizens.

CHAMA TODAY

Located in a gorgeous part of northern New Mexico, only eight miles from the Colorado border, Chama is largely a tourist community, dependent on visitors who come to the tiny town especially during the fall season to ride the Cumbres & Toltec Scenic Railroad and to enjoy vivid fall leaves. The authentic steam engine winds sixty-four miles along the narrow rails placed in 1880 from Chama, New Mexico, to Antonito, Colorado—the original line of the Denver and Rio Grande Railroad. This railway is the longest three-and-a-half-foot-wide narrow-gauge route in the United States. The trek takes six and a half hours and includes lunch. The train travels six hundred feet over the Rio Chama in spots, traversing two tunnels and one hundred feet of trestle along the way.

The Cumbres & Toltec Scenic Railroad is a registered state and national historic site. It is designated a National Civil Engineering Landmark by the American Society of Civil Engineers. The railway was recently voted one of the twenty best railway experiences in the world by the Society of International Railway Travelers. During the six-and-a-half-hour ride, the Cumbres & Toltec Scenic Railroad crosses back and forth from New Mexico to Colorado eleven times.

Diversity is abundant in Chama, as the Spanish, Native and Anglo cultures coexist without strife. Many new residents seek a respite from the ant-bed societies of the larger cities, escaping to the crisp, clear air and solitude of the high-country village. Many open quaint shops and cafés. The small community is only one hundred miles north of Santa Fe on Highway 84. Chama has been the setting for several movies, including *Butch and Sundance: The Early Days* (1979), *The Good Guys and the Bad Guys* (1969) and *Bite the Bullet* (1975).

The main street in Chama runs parallel to the railroad tracks, surrounded on both sides by aspen and pine trees. Sculptures of elk pay homage to the

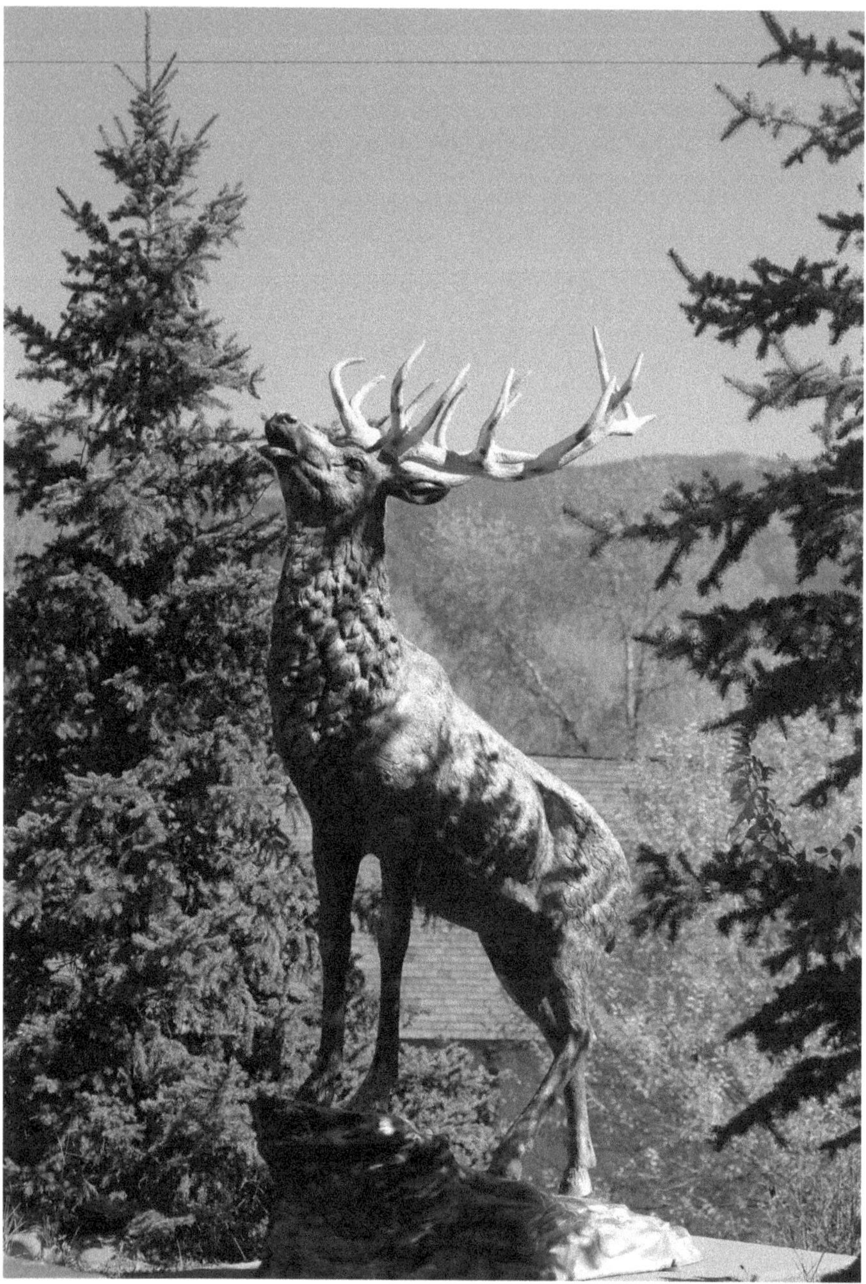

The quiet street running through Chama is dotted with hotels, cabins, gift shops and cafés. Shimmering aspens beg you to sit and take in the beauty. *Courtesy of the author.*

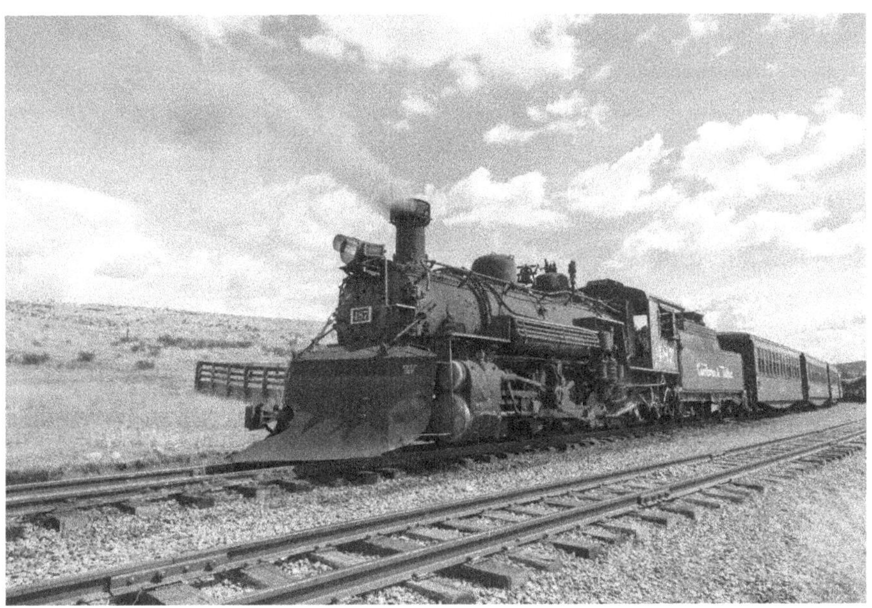

The Cumbres & Toltec Railroad has been voted one of the top ten scenic railways in the world. *Library of Congress.*

magnificent beasts that are prevalent in the region. With a population of around twelve hundred, Chama sits in a picturesque part of northern New Mexico along the Rio Chama at an elevation of 7,860 feet. The Colorado border is a mere seven miles from Chama; for those who enjoy jaw-dropping, vibrant green countryside and awe-inspiring views, this is the landscape.

Many parks, cabins, restaurants and shops await visitors. The theme of Chama is most definitely tied to the railroad, and rightfully so, since it is such an important aspect of the region. Chama's motto is "All roads lead to Chama." Chama is set in a historic valley that is diverse in cultures and stretches from the Colorado border to the Tierra Amarilla Valley and as far south as Abiquiu, which inspired the stunning artworks of Georgia O'Keeffe. The town likes to promote itself as a great venue for reunions, weddings and hunting parties.

Like many mountain communities in New Mexico, the exquisite beauty that surrounds the town has attracted artists who set up studios and give art tours. In 2017, there were sixteen artist studios on the tour.

Foster's Hotel & Restaurant

Built in 1880, Foster's Hotel and Restaurant is the oldest commercial structure in the village of Chama. Conveniently located across the street from the Cumbres & Toltec railyard, Foster's was and is the place to stay after riding the rails. With a full-service saloon and restaurant that are open seven days a week, Foster's Hotel is a wonderful place to relax after a long day of sightseeing.

Foster's Hotel has seen continuous expansions and improvements since 1932 and was one of two hotels in the town. Although Chama suffered a series of devastating fires over the years, Foster's Hotel has been spared. The other hotel was not so lucky. The owners like to think of their hotel and restaurant as a living piece of history and are enthusiastic to talk about it.

As with other hotels featured in this book, Foster's Hotel was once a Harvey House, serving the workers and passengers of the Denver and Rio Grande Railroad. It was once owned by Alice Nuño, who purchased Foster's Hotel in 1979 and did a complete restoration of the dilapidated building, bringing it back to life while preserving the historical value as well.

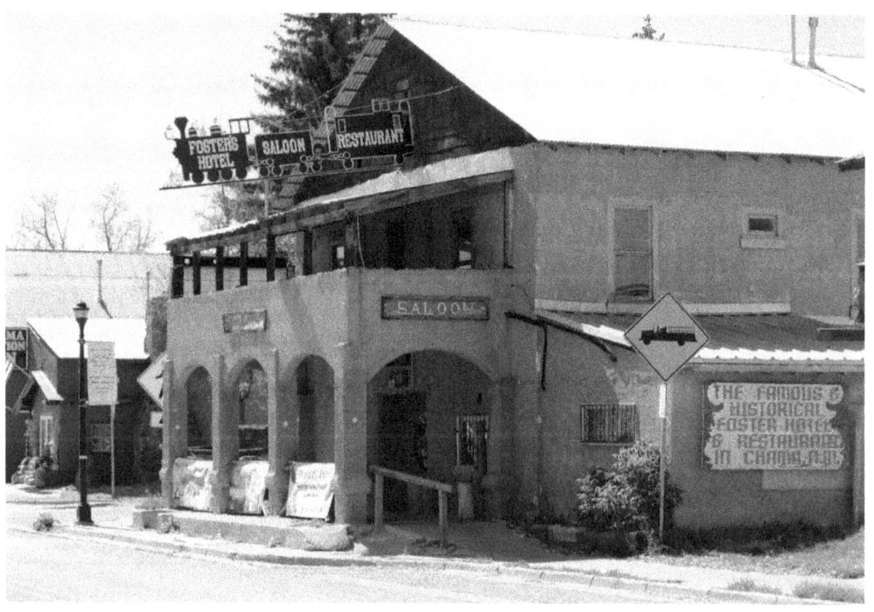

Foster's Inn in Chama, New Mexico, is the oldest commercial building in town. *Courtesy of the author.*

The hotel, in Rio Arriba County, is in the National Register of Historic Places. Constructed of adobe and railroad ties, Foster's Hotel is a distinctive landmark on the corner of Fourth and Terrace in Chama.

Ghosts

Guests at Foster's Hotel have reported hearing a woman coughing and gasping in the hallway—it was thought to have been the final sounds of a newly elected female judge in the 1800s who was poisoned at the hotel. It is said that she was poisoned by the men of the town, who did not like a woman as judge. She was found dead the next day.

The cries of a young girl who reportedly died from an illness more than one hundred years ago in one of the Foster's Hotel rooms have upset staff and patrons alike. It is also reported that this ghost likes to rattle doorknobs.

Distinctive sounds of a cowboy's jingling spurs pacing the second-floor hallway have sent many guests to the front desk to ask what they were hearing.

A dark shadow has been reported in room 21, possibly the same spirit, and guests have noticed cold and hot spots in room 25.

Service staff have reported a spirit that likes to unmake beds and throw blankets on the floor after the beds have been made.

10
HATCH/RODEY

HISTORIC HATCH/RODEY

The early Spanish explorers settled in the Hatch Valley in the late 1500s to early 1600s, establishing Rodey, the oldest village in the area, and Hatch as an agricultural sector of New Mexico. The Hatch/Rodey area relied on the backbreaking efforts of farmworkers who toiled for countless hours in the onion, corn, cotton, alfalfa, lettuce, cabbage, oats and, especially, chile fields, as well as pecan orchards.

Established in 1865, Rodey was originally named Colorado, which means "red," after the color of the cliffs that surround the area. The name was later changed in honor of an Irish immigrant from County Mayo, Bernard Shandon Rodey, who came to Albuquerque to work as a stenographer for the A&P Railroad but later served as New Mexico's territorial delegate to the U.S. Congress. Rodey, a prominent attorney and legislator, was instrumental in founding the University of New Mexico, along with help from Judge John R. McFie. Rodey is now known as the "Father of the University" through the Rodey Act of 1889.

In the early days, Rodey saw turmoil, since it was once walled as a defense against the Apache tribe that roamed the area and the John Kinney outlaw gang. (Kinney had been a participant in the Lincoln County War and was shot in the face by Billy the Kid but survived to tell the tale.) The gang stole thousands of head of cattle from local ranchers, driving the cattle to

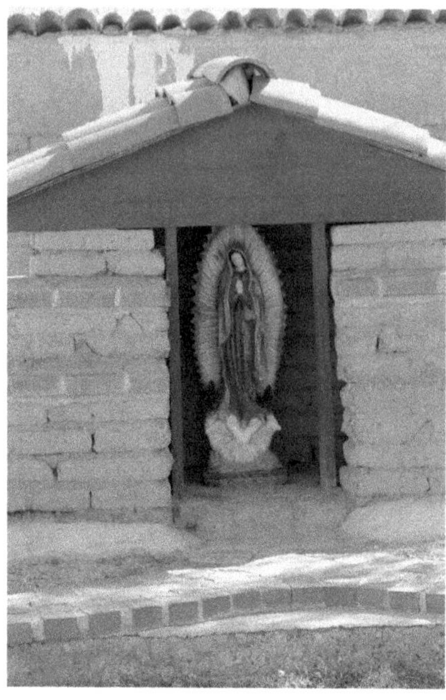

The shrine to Our Lady of Guadalupe in the courtyard of the St. Francis de Sales Church also holds the cremains of a former owner. *Courtesy of the author.*

slaughter across the Rio Grande to Rincon, New Mexico, a neighboring colonia of Hatch. Apache chief Victorio and his band stole local horses for his tribe to use as well as trade.

Rodey was a railroad community, the hub of the region in the late 1800s, until the railroad was moved northwest of the town, making Hatch the boomtown. As the population of Hatch increased, the population of Rodey decreased. St. Francis de Sales Church served as the major religious center for the population until 1963, when a new church, Our Lady of Mercy, was constructed in Hatch, drawing away the majority of St. Francis's parishioners. It was then that the decision to deconsecrate St. Francis de Sales was made and the transfer of the parish seat was given to Hatch.

The construction of Elephant Butte Dam in 1917 established the Hatch Valley as an agricultural stronghold, as irrigation was then available.

HATCH/RODEY TODAY

Nestled three miles southeast of Hatch, New Mexico, which was originally named Santa Barbara, is the tiny farming village of Rodey, a colonia of

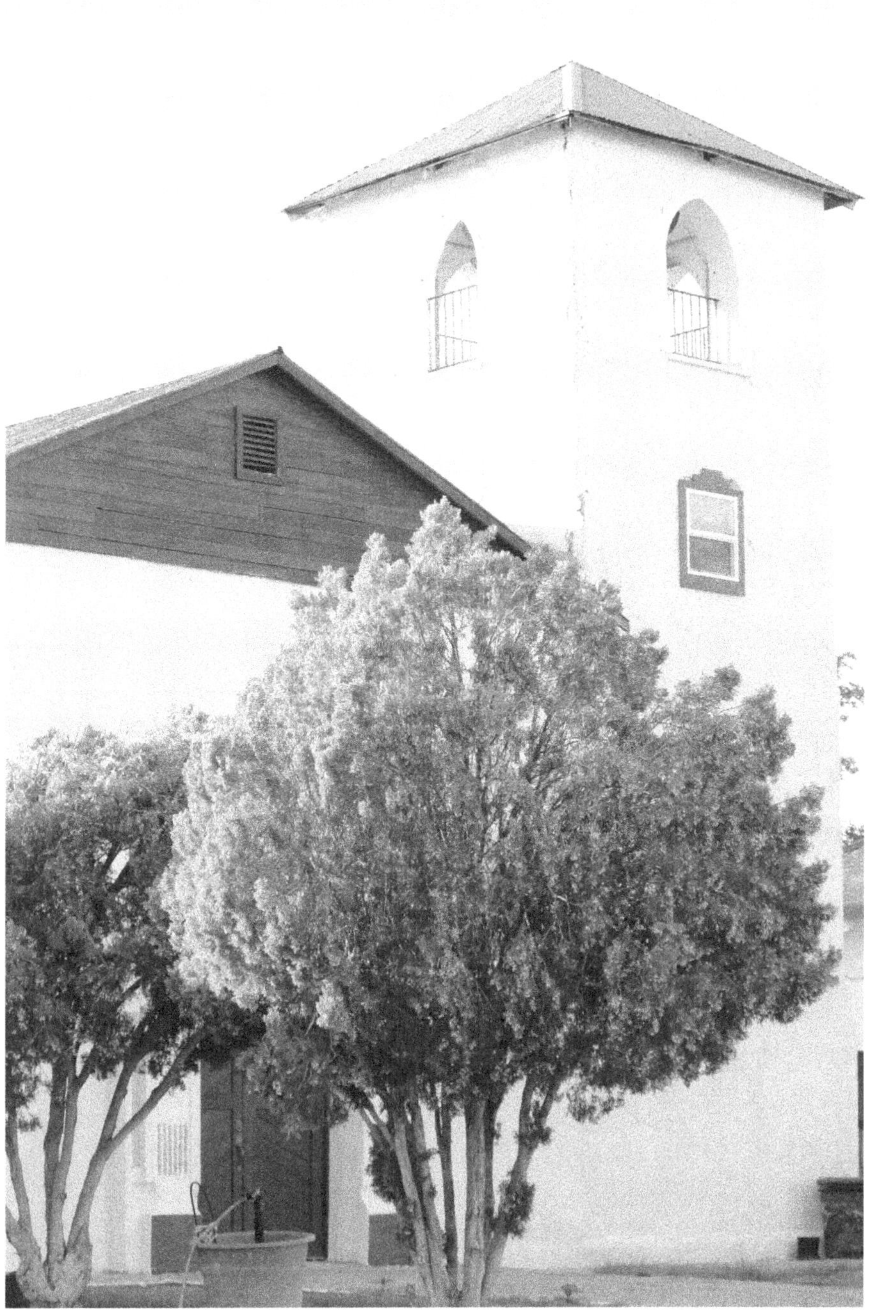

The fully restored St. Francis de Sales Church is the hub of the community and still serves as a religious gathering point. *Courtesy of the author.*

Hatch. At its center is St. Francis de Sales Church. Rodey is a poor community of farmers who mainly make their living working in the surrounding chile fields. The chile has made modern-day Hatch famous throughout the world.

New Mexicans can hardly wait for August to roll around, for that means the chile harvest is finally at hand. The air is filled with the heady aroma of roasting green chile—in the opinion of nearly every New Mexican, it is better than any perfume on the market! Hatch, with a population of approximately seventeen hundred people and a mere thirty-seven miles from Las Cruces, is credited with putting the glorious green chile on the radar for the world, as it has proclaimed itself to be the Chile Capital of the World. New Mexico is so proud of the chile, a new license plate has been developed, allowing everyone to display chile pride.

As a small, close-knit community, Rodey still celebrates the holy days and feast days of the church by holding processions and fiestas in honor of the saints. The priest from nearby Hatch performs religious rites by blessing each home in Rodey and praying for the occupants, with nearly every citizen in tow. St. Francis de Sales Church is still a vital part of this community.

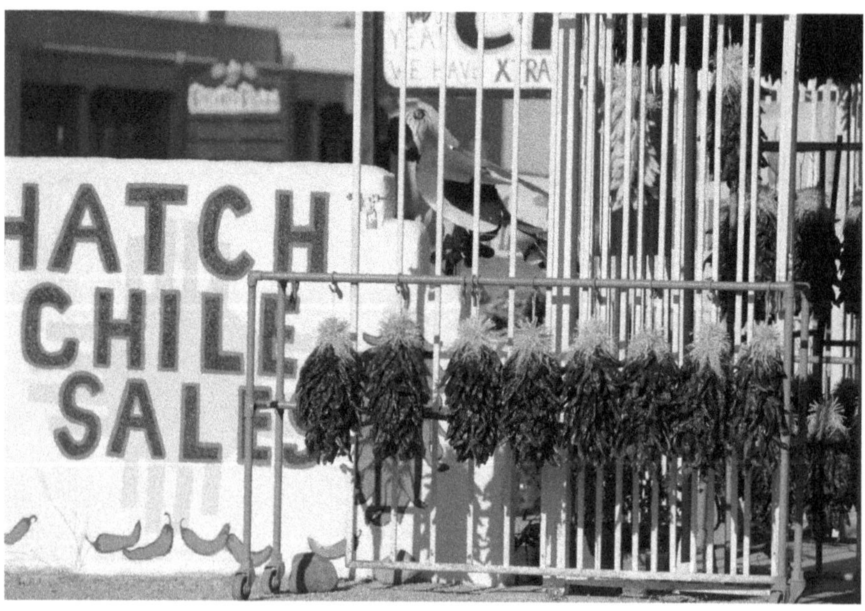

Hatch, New Mexico, is the Chile Capital of the World and has the sign to prove it! *Courtesy of the author.*

St. Francis de Sales Church, Events, Retreats and Suites

Construction began on St. Francis de Sales Church in 1860 by the Diocese of Tucson. It would take twenty-five years for it to be completed. Flooding from the Rio Grande in 1870 caused the church to be rebuilt when the entire community was forced to move farther west, to its current location. Later, when St. Francis became a mission of St. Genevieve (Las Cruces Diocese), it began keeping written records.

With its eighteen-inch-thick walls fashioned out of the traditional adobe brick in the shape of a cross, and its twelve-foot ceilings, the church has taken a long, arduous journey from humble beginnings to the retreat it is today. Co-owner Alice Marley was proud to point out that the windows in the bathrooms of the main house were fashioned with deep angles of wall surrounding them, since they were once used in defense of the building from the raids by the Apaches, and this style gave a better vantage point.

Locally harvested logs dictated the thirty-foot width of the nave. The two-foot walls of the bell tower were restored in 1963. The tower now

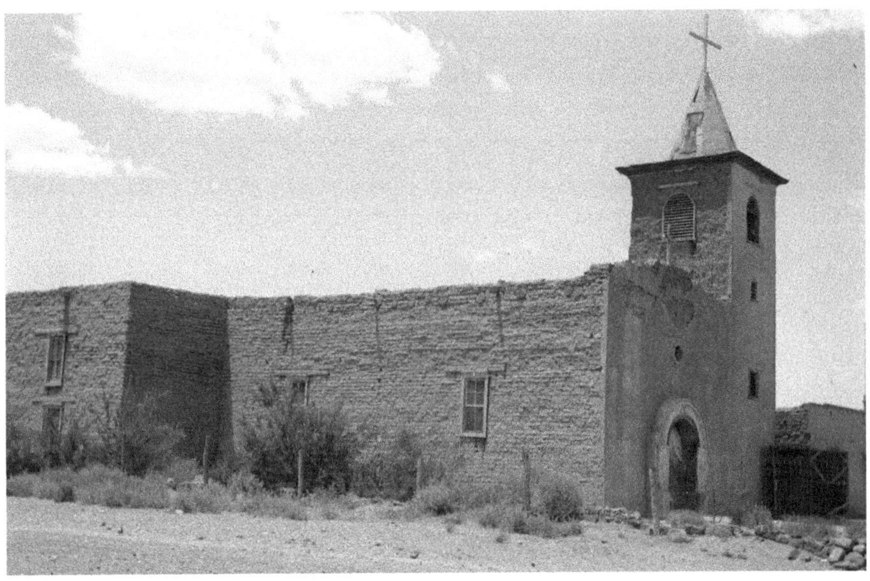

The humble beginning of St. Francis de Sales Church is evident in this image. The adobe structure has been covered with stucco for stability and preservation. *Library of Congress.*

provides some of the best views of the valley. These restorations landed the church in the New Mexico State Historical Register. The current owners, Celeste Zimmerman and Alice Marley, have taken the church artifacts that remained and had not been taken to Our Lady of All Nations Church in nearby Rincon during the many turnovers the property saw throughout the years, and returned the church back, as close as possible, to the original configuration. Antique wooden pews, altar railing and statuary have given the church a sanctified character. No matter man's status in this church, God still resides there, and His presence is deeply felt.

An outdoor kiva fireplace with grill sets the mood for gatherings and celebrations. The owners have recounted times when they have returned home to the church to find large, impromptu family reunions happening on their patio. Alice was quick to note how happy she is that the community has embraced them and their mission, as they school the easterners on the ways of New Mexico.

St. Francis de Sales is the patron saint of writers, editors and publishers. He is also credited with developing a form of sign language he used to convert a deaf man to Catholicism, as well as writing many inspirational books. Born to an aristocratic family in Thorens, France, in 1567, Francis dedicated his life and prayers to helping the poor as he lived a very simple life. The eldest of six sons, Francis studied law, theology and the humanities, but he gave up a chance for a law career to follow his calling.

After suffering a stroke, Francis de Sales died on December 28, 1622, at the age of fifty-six. He was beatified in 1661, canonized by Pope Alexander VII in 1665 and declared a Doctor of the Universal Church by Pope Pius IX in 1877.

The retreat and suites is located in the original twenty-three-hundred-square-foot rectory. Each room is decorated with a mixture of Middle Eastern/Southwestern flair by co-owner Celeste Zimmerman. The welcome you will receive by these two hardworking ladies will warm your heart and have you wishing you never had to leave. Saltillo tile covers the floors throughout the building, complementing the white plastered walls, fireplaces and ceilings highlighted by vigas, latillas and exposed beams. Also available is a large casita, which shares a wall with the church. Used as an art studio by previous owners, this ample room, which sleeps five, provides serenity and offers a kitchenette, woodstove, separate bath and a private entrance.

An early-morning tea or a cup of coffee under the pergola in the courtyard will be certain to start your day off right. The owners are delightful people who want to meet their guests' every need. As one of the first guests, I can

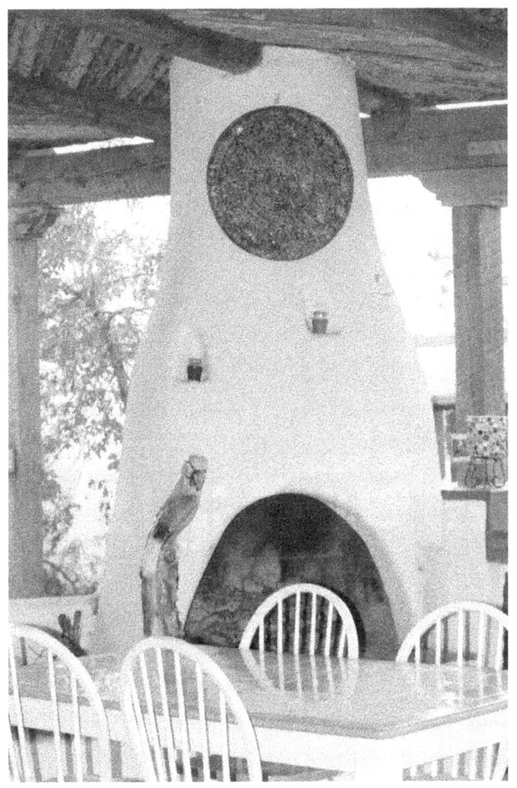

Left: The outdoor patio area of St. Francis de Sales Church has seen many festivals and celebrations and continues to be the hub of the community. *Courtesy of the author.*

Below: A large casita available to rent was once used as an artist's studio and has accommodations for five with kitchen facilities. *Courtesy of the author.*

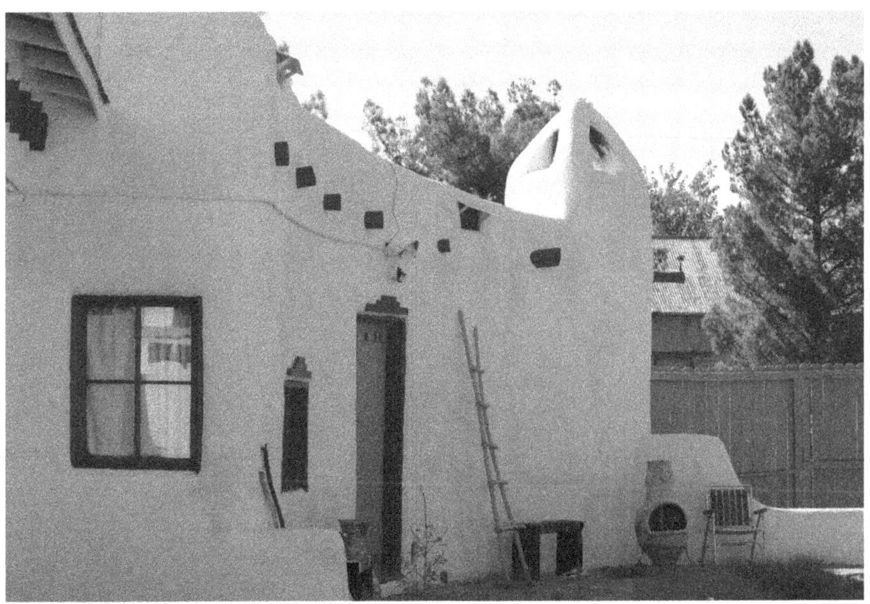

highly recommend this retreat and hope to return soon for another visit, since I felt less like a guest and more like family during my short stay.

Saint Francis de Sales Events, Retreats and Suites provides a perfect venue for weddings. The wooden gazebo in the courtyard can be beautifully decorated to suit any wedding style, and the casita makes for a wonderfully romantic and private honeymoon suite. St. Francis also hosts family reunions, class reunions, community celebrations and feast days as well as providing a relaxing retreat for small parties who want to get away from the rat race of the city.

The main house (former rectory) features a cozy reception room and kitchen space right off the outdoor patio area, so guests can lounge, check e-mail or watch a movie. A walk through the grounds will bring solace to a weary soul.

Included in the sale of the church was a Carillon Bell System, which was used to ring out for masses, funerals and celebrations. The new owners are carrying on these traditions, as beautiful music is once again played for special occasions. According to Josie Nunn, previous owner of the property, they used to play "Home on the Range" by means of a player piano in the church. Because of these bells ringing, the community gathered and eventually formed a group, which led to the restoration of roads and a new community center in Rodey. The bell tower is also available for the adventurous to spend the night.

The Silva family has strong roots in Rodey and with St. Francis de Sales Church; in fact, the street that runs in front of the church is names Jesus Silva Street. Many of the family were baptized, married and had their funerals in this church, so, recently, Ed Silva handcrafted a large, carved wooden cross to hang over the altar. The cross is proudly displayed as a beautiful symbol of faith. Such gestures warm the hearts of the owners and make them feel like they are part of the family.

Ghosts

Given the age and history of St. Francis de Sales Church, it is not surprising to have tales of spiritual encounters. After all, there are four known burials on the property. With that said, the ambiance of the retreat is extremely peaceful. Unless you are extremely sensitive to the spirit world, you would never be aware of the more permanent residents. Three of these burials are nearly 150 years old.

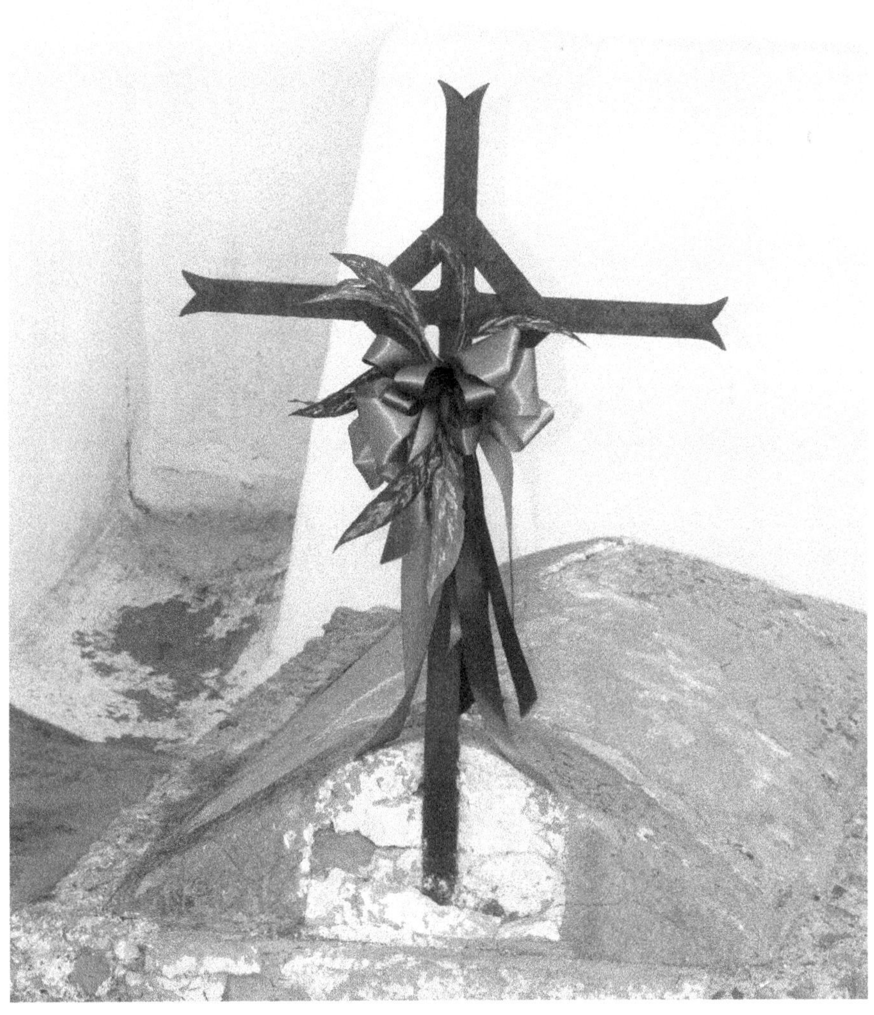

This is a lone concrete-covered grave of a Gypsy boy who was buried here at his parents' request. He is a playful spirit around the guests. *Courtesy of the author.*

Two young priests, possibly brothers, now rest under the floor to the left of the altar, which was customary in their time. According to church records, one of the young men was said to have been murdered and the other fell victim to a severe illness. Images of shadows have been captured. Odd happenings, such as flickering lights, rushes of cold air and slamming doors, sometimes take place within the church, leading some to think these are the actions of the deceased priests.

The other burial is outside in the churchyard, and it is not a burial at all, but a scattering of ashes. The father of one of the former recent owners wanted his ashes scattered on the property after his death, so he was obliged, and his ashes now rest at the shrine to Our Lady of Guadalupe. His spirit is also thought to spend time gently rocking in a chair on the front porch of the casita.

It is the next burial that is the most tragic and heartbreaking—that of a fifteen-year-old Romany boy, thought to be named Elias, who was accidently shot, possibly by his brother, in the late 1880s. As they were only traveling through, his grieving parents brought the young boy to the priest at St. Francis de Sales Church to ask if they could bury him on the church grounds. Their request was granted, and the small grave of young Elias is now just below

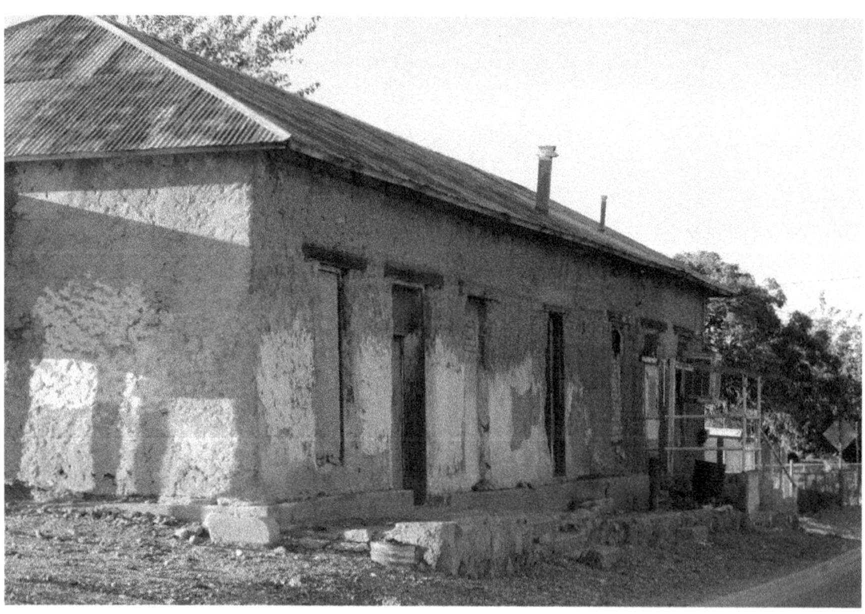

Directly behind St. Francis de Sales is a former saloon that made its television debut in 2015 on *American Pickers*. *Courtesy of the author.*

a window of the church in the courtyard behind the bell tower. The grave, which is encased in cement with a handcrafted iron cross as a headstone, is a sad reminder of the hardships families encountered during their travels across this country in search of a better life. Elias's spirit is thought to be mischievous and has been reported to peer into windows or cause doors to slam or items to move. These are harmless pranks of youth, but it can rattle the nerves.

A figure of a man dressed in priest's robes has also been reported to walk through the casita in a procession to the church sacristy—a harmless residual memory of the past.

Across the street from the church is an old, dilapidated adobe building that housed a lively saloon in the late 1800s, then saw life as a meeting place for the local Veterans of Foreign Wars (VFW). It now serves as storage for a former owner of St. Francis de Sales and was featured on the popular cable television show *American Pickers*. During its life as a saloon, many gunfights occurred in and around the vicinity, including in the courtyard of the church. Bullets were found encased in the adobe walls when the church was restored. Local legend has it that residents hear these gunfights playing out once again on clear summer evenings.

No matter the residents, St. Francis de Sales Church is still a sacred, serene location that will renew your soul and provide you with the peace you desire.

BIBLIOGRAPHY

Balcomb, Kenneth C. *A Boy's Albuquerque, 1898–1912*. Albuquerque: University of New Mexico Press, 1980.

Billington, Monroe Lee. *New Mexico's Buffalo Soldiers: 1866–1900*. Niwot: University of Colorado, 1991.

Birchell, Donna Blake. *Carlsbad and Carlsbad Caverns*. Charleston, SC: Arcadia Publishing, 2010.

———. *New Mexico Wine: An Enchanting History*. Charleston, SC: The History Press, 2013.

———. *Wicked Women of New Mexico*. Charleston, SC: The History Press, 2014.

Blumenthal, S. *Santa Fe Ghosts: Mystery, History and Truth.* Atglen, PA: Schiffer Publishing, 2009.

Bryan, Howard. *Albuquerque Remembered.* Albuquerque: University of New Mexico Press, 2006.

———. *Wildest of the Wild West: True Tales of a Frontier Town on the Santa Fe Trail.* Santa Fe, NM: Clear Light Publishing Co., 1988.

Caffey, David L. *Frank Springer & New Mexico: From the Colfax County War to the Emergence of Modern Santa Fe.* College Station: Texas A&M University Press, 2007.

Caldwell, Clifford R. *Dead Right: The Lincoln County War*. Kerrville, TX: self-published, 2008.

———. *John Simpson Chisum: Cattle King of the Pecos Revisited.* Santa Fe, NM: Sunstone Press, 2010.

Cedrins, Inara. *Albuquerque Ghosts: Traditions, Legends and Lore*. Atglen, PA: Schiffer Publishing, 2009.

Crutchfield, James A. *Revolt at Taos: The New Mexican and Indian Insurrection of 1847*. Yardley, PA: Westholme Publishing, 2015.

Fergusson, Erna. *Erna Fergusson's Albuquerque*. Albuquerque, NM: Merle Armitage Editions, 1947.

Frazier, Donald S. *Blood & Treasure: Confederate Empire in the Southwest*. College Station: Texas A&M University Press, 1997.

Fulton, Maurice G. *History of the Lincoln County War: A Classic Account of Billy the Kid*. Tucson: University of Arizona Press, 1997.

Garcez, Antonio R. *New Mexico Ghost Stories*. Rockledge, FL: Red Rabbit Press, 2003.

———. *New Mexico Ghost Stories, Vol. II*, Rockledge, FL: Red Rabbit Press, 2014.

Harrelson, Barbara. *From Every Window: A Glimpse of the Past*. Santa Fe, NM: La Fonda de Santa Fe, 2011.

Harris, Richard. *New Mexico off the Beaten Path: A Guide to Unique Places*. 9th ed. Guilford, CT: Globe Pequot Press, 2010.

Hooker, Van Dorn, with Melissa Howard and Vincent B. Price. *Only in New Mexico: An Architectural History of the University of New Mexico: The First Century, 1889–1989*. 1st ed. Albuquerque: University of New Mexico Press, 2000.

Horn, Calvin. *New Mexico's Troubled Years: The Story of the Early Territorial Governors*. Albuquerque, NM: Horn & Wallace, 1963.

Johnson, Byron A. *Old Town, Albuquerque, New Mexico: A Guide to Its History and Architecture*. Albuquerque, NM: City of Albuquerque, 1980.

Keleher, William A. *The Fabulous Frontier: Twelve New Mexico Items*. Santa Fe, NM: Rydal Press, 1945.

———. *Turmoil in New Mexico: 1846–1868*. Albuquerque: University of New Mexico Press, 1982.

LeMay, John. *Tall Tales and Half Truths of Billy the Kid*. Charleston, SC: The History Press, 2015.

———. *Tall Tales and Half Truths of Pat Garrett*. Charleston, SC: The History Press, 2016.

———. *Towns of Lincoln County*. Charleston, SC: Arcadia Publishing, 2010.

Londene, Carl and Donna. *Call the Vet*. Mustang, OK: Tate Publishing & Enterprises, 2012.

Looney, Ralph. *Haunted Highways: The Ghost Towns of New Mexico.* New York: Hastings House, 1968.

Luhan, Mabel Dodge. *Edge of Taos Desert: An Escape to Reality*. New York: Harcourt, Brace, 1937.

Lynn, Sandra D. *Windows on the Past: Historic Lodgings of New Mexico.* Albuquerque: University of New Mexico Press, 1999.

McKenna, James A. *Black Range Tales.* Chicago: Rio Grande Press, 1965.

Metz, Leon C. *Pat Garrett: The Story of a Western Lawman*. Norman: University of Oklahoma Press, 1973.

Murphy, Lawrence R. *Philmont: A History of New Mexico's Cimarron Country.* Albuquerque: University of New Mexico Press, 1972.

Nordhaus, Hannah. *American Ghost: A Family's Extraordinary History on the Desert Frontier*. New York: Harper Perennial, 2016.

Osterwald, Doris B. *Ticket to Toltec: A Mile by Mile Guide for the Cumbres & Toltec Scenic Railroad*. Hugo, CO: Western Guideways, 2002.

Pappas, Mike J. *Raton: History, Mystery and More.* Raton, NM: Coda Publications, 2003.

Polston, Cody. *Ghosts of Old Town Albuquerque*. Charleston, SC: The History Press, 2012

Radford, Benjamin. *Mysteries New Mexico: Miracles, Magic & Monsters in the Land of Enchantment*. Albuquerque: University of New Mexico Press, 2014.

Raisch, Bruce. *Haunted Hotels of the West.* Virginia Beach, VA: Donning Company, 2009.

Rakocy, Bill. *Ghosts of Kingston Hillsboro.* El Paso, TX: Bravo Press, 1983.

Rojas, Eileen Vanessa. "Cultural Intersections and Historic Preservations: A Study of Las Vegas, New Mexico." Master's thesis (historic preservation), University of Pennsylvania, Philadelphia, 2014.

Romancito, M. Elwell. *Ghosts & Haunted Places of Taos.* Taos, NM: Romancito House Media, 2015.

Rudnick, Lois. *Mabel Dodge Luhan: New Woman, New Worlds*. Albuquerque: University of New Mexico Press, 1996.

Sherman, James. *Ghost Towns and Mining Camps of New Mexico.* Norman: University of Oklahoma Press, 1975.

Silverman, J. *Untold New Mexico: Stories from a Hidden Past.* Santa Fe, NM: Sunstone Press, 2006.

Simmons, Marc. *Albuquerque: A Narrative History*. Albuquerque: University of New Mexico Press, 1982.

Thompson, Jerry. *Civil War in the Southwest: Recollection of the Sibley Brigade.* College Station: Texas A&M University Press, 2001.

Twitchell, Ralph Emmerson. *The Leading Facts of New Mexico History.* Cedar Rapids, IA: Torch Press, 1911.

Utley, Robert M. *High Noon in Lincoln: Violence on the Western Frontier.* Albuquerque: University of New Mexico Press, 1987.

Varney, Philip. *New Mexico's Best Ghost Towns: A Practical Guide*. Albuquerque: University of New Mexico Press, 1987.

Weigles, Marta. *Alluring New Mexico: Engineered Enchantment, 1821–2001*. Santa Fe: Museum of New Mexico Press, 2010.

Whitford, William C. *Colorado Volunteers in the Civil War: The New Mexico Campaign in 1862*. Glorieta, NM: Rio Grande Press, 1994.

Whitlock, Flint. *Distant Bugles, Distant Drums: The Union Response to the Confederate Invasion of New Mexico*. Boulder: University Press of Colorado, 2006.

Williams, Nancy K. *Haunted Hotels of the California Gold Country*. Charleston, SC: The History Press, 2014.

Wilson, John P. *Merchants, Guns & Money: The Story of Lincoln County and Its Wars*. Santa Fe: Museum of New Mexico Press, 1987.

———. *Pat Garrett and Billy the Kid as I Knew Them: Reminiscences of John P. Meadows*. Albuquerque: University of New Mexico Press, 2004.

———. *When the Texans Came: Missing Records from the Civil War in the Southwest. 1861–1862*. Albuquerque: University of New Mexico Press, 2001.

Internet Resources

Haunted Places. www.hauntedplaces.org.

Legends of America. www.legendsofamerica.com.

New Mexico History. New Mexico State Historian. www.newmexicohistory.org.

Southwest Ghost Hunters Association. www.sgha.net.

Hotel Websites and Contact Information

Crow's Nest Bed & Breakfast
www.thecrowsnestbandb.com
524 Columbia
Las Vegas, New Mexico 87701
(505) 425-2623

Dolan House
www.thedolanhouse.com
826 Calle la Placita (Highway 380)
Lincoln, New Mexico 88338
(575) 653-4670

Express St. James Hotel
www.exstjames.com
617 S. Collison Avenue
Cimarron, New Mexico 87714
(575) 376-2664

Foster's Hotel and Restaurant
www.fosters1881.com
393 Terrace Avenue
Chama, New Mexico 87520
(575) 756-2296

Hacienda Del Sol
www.taoshaciendadelsol.com
109 Mabel Dodge Lane
Taos, New Mexico 87551
(575) 758-0287

La Fonda on the Plaza
www.lafondasantafe.com
100 East San Francisco Street
Santa Fe, New Mexico 87501
(505) 988-2952

Laguna Vista Lodge
www.lagunavistalodge.com
51 East Therma Drive
Eagle Nest, New Mexico 87718
(575) 377-6522

La Posada de Santa Fe
www.laposadadesantafe.com
330 East Palace Avenue
Santa Fe, New Mexico 87501
(505) 986-0000

The Painted Lady Bed & Brew
1100 Bellamah Avenue Northwest
Albuquerque, New Mexico 87104
(505) 200-3999

Plaza Hotel
www.plazahotellvnm.com
230 Plaza
Las Vegas, New Mexico 87701
(505) 425-3591

Red Horse Vineyard Bed & Breakfast
www.redhorsebb.com
2155 Londene Lane Southwest
Albuquerque, New Mexico 87105
(505) 967-7610

St. Francis de Sales Church, Events, Retreat and Suites
https://www.facebook.com/pages/Saint-Francis-de-Sales-Church-Historic-Site/1055578328348747hc_ref=ARQLxinutQecbu0121gFJC8gqYaHeZPE3kigjXOIptpAKz94dVdaj38KUIuMuEqb8vY
105 North Jose Serna Street
Hatch, New Mexico 87937
(712) 420-5719

The Trinity Hotel
www.thetrinityhotel.com
201 North Canal Street
Carlsbad, New Mexico 88220
(575) 234-9891

The Wortley Hotel
www.wortleyhotel.com
585 Calle la Placita (Hwy. 380)
Lincoln, New Mexico 88338
(575) 653-4300

INDEX

Q

R

S

Z

About the Author

Donna Blake Birchell is a native of the Land of Enchantment. Although Donna has traveled to and lived in many states, her heart always brings her back to New Mexico. Her career as a library cataloger gave her a great love of books, with which she surrounds herself at every chance. When she was a child, her father, William Blake, instilled in her a love of history as he performed a lengthy travelogue during their weekend travels throughout New Mexico and Texas.

Writing is a passion that began early for Donna, as she wrote her first short story at age twelve. As the author of seven books featuring New Mexico and Texas, she has a dream to bring the fascinating history of her beloved region to as many readers as possible, so they may also marvel at the sheer magnitude of the stories still untold. Recently, photography has gripped her soul, providing another much-needed creative outlet that complements her books perfectly.

The thrill of finding additional information during research, hearing a fresh take on an old story and being able to play detective in unearthing new clues into the rich history of the area is what keeps Donna striving to continue on this fantastic journey.

Donna's proudest accomplishments are her two sons, who live in New Mexico and Texas—much too far, in her opinion, from her Carlsbad home.

www.ingramcontent.com/pod-product-compliance
Lightning Source LLC
LaVergne TN
LVHW052341100826
845147LV00021B/1144

* 9 7 8 1 4 6 7 1 3 8 8 9 5 *